VA and AFGE

GUIDE TO INNER UNDERSTANDING

Brain-Heart Coherence

LESSONS LEARNED
LESSONS TAUGHT

Brain-heart coherence is a state of unity between the mind, body, and spirit, where the brainwaves and the heart's electrical activity are in sync. It can have many benefits, including:

- Improved emotional stability
- Increased creativity
- Better decision-making
- Greater clarity of thought
- Improved sleep quality
- Reduced stress levels
- Increased physical energy
- Greater resilience
- Improved physical health

VINCET VIRES VIRTUS
VIRTUE CONQUERS FORCE

© 2023 by Richard L. Matteoli

No part of this book may be reproduced by any mechanical, photographic, or electronic process, or in the form of a phonographic record, nor may it be stored in a retrieval system, transmitted, or otherwise be copied for public or private use – other than for "fair use" as brief quotations embodied in articles and reviews – without prior written permission of the publisher.

Nemean Press™
First Conquer Thyself
Primo Evinco Te
Richard L. Matteoli

A Guide to inner understanding as a:
Ethics Workbook for Brain-Heart Coherence:

VA and AFGE
LESSONS LEARNED – LESSONS TAUGHT

Soft Cover ISBN: 978-1-943347-11-5

Acknowledgment: John J. Whitworth

TABLE OF CONTENTS

INTRODUCTION
4

CODES OF CONDUCT
6

ETHICS
7

DEFINITIONS
11

CONDITIONS
17

BEHAVIORS
21

COMMUNICATION
23

INTSTRUCTIONS
26

WORKSHEETS
30

INTRODUCTION

(Brain-Logos-Scientific)
Investigate what is, and not what pleases.
Goethe. *The Attempt as Mediator of Object and Object.*

Everyone has a Wounded Child. It usually begins around the ages of 6 to 8. More likely than not it involves a member of the opposite sex regardless of the perpetrator's age.

It occurs in a social event, that is to say other people usually know though not everyone. It brings to you the feeling of an injustice has happened to you. The main factor is a sense of humiliation.

You may have already thought of yours. This event lives inside you for your entire lifetime. It will form a basis of how you sense justice and relates to how you react to situations in every-day life.

A

Sacred Contracts written by Carolyn Myss regarding the Wounded Child and other unconscious Child Archetypes as the Prostitute, Destroyer and Caretaker would be beneficial.

B

Anima and Animus by Emma Jung, Carl Jung's wife, would be an extremely useful adjunct.

C

Ritual Theory, Ritual Practice by Catherine Bell is useful to understand social Team Predation.

D

Texts by FBI Criminal Profilers John Douglas, Mark Olshaker, Robert Ressler, Roy Hazelwood and Ann Burgess will aid understanding behavior, though that behavior does not relate in actual death, but the actions were meant to put a stop, or create a situation, to some perplexing subject.

(Heart-Eros-Artistic)
Investigation is implied in our Mandate
Anakin Skywalker. *Attack of the Clones.*

LOGOS: Logos is a rhetorical device that uses logic and evidence to support a claim or argument.

EROS: Eros was the Greek god of love, or more precisely, passionate and physical desire. Without warning Eros selects his targets and forcefully strikes at their hearts, bringing confusion and irrepressible feelings.

The concept of Eros could be expressed in modern terms as psychic relatedness, and that of Logos as objective interest. This gendering of eros and logos is a consequence of Jung's theory of the anima/animus syzygy of the human psyche.

As a general guide Lessons Learned will tend to be more from Logos whereas Lessons Taught will tend to be more from Eros.

CODES OF CONDUCT

Laws control the lesser man.
Right conduct controls the greater one.
Mark Twain.

A Code of Conduct is a set of rules outlining the social norms and rules and responsibilities of, or proper practices for, an individual, party or organization. There are 8 norms of conduct for public officials and employees:

Commitment to Public Interest

Professionalism

Justice and Sincerity

Political Neutrality

Responsiveness to the Public

Nationalism and Patriotism

Commitment to Democracy

Simple Living

Let them hate me,
provided they respect my conduct.
Tiberius.

ETHICS

A man without ethics is a wild beast loosed upon this world.
Albert Camus

ETHICS: **1.** Moral principles that govern a person's behavior or the conducting of an activity. **2.** The branch of knowledge that deals with moral principles.

MORAL: of or relating to principles of right and wrong in behavior: ethical expressing or teaching a conception of right behavior.

ALTRUISTIC ETHOS: a postulated form of argument or discussion to enhance a belief or position as it relates to humanity in general

SELECTIVE ETHOS: a postulated form of argument or discussion to enhance a belief or position that usually separates one person or group of persons from another person or group of persons usually via perceived innate differences between them, and often contains deceptions from altruistic posturing with subsequent actions in Situation Ethics, which is a Fallacy.

SITUATIONAL ETHICS: the doctrine of flexibility in the application of moral laws according to circumstances.

SUPERNATURALISM: a belief in an otherworldly realm or reality that, in one way or another, is commonly associated with all forms of religion.

SUBJECTIVISM: Subjectivism in ethics suggests that moral statements are only ever the opinion and experience of the person saying the statement, and collective moral opinions come about when many people agree on ethical matters.

CONSEQUENTIALISM: Consequentialism is an ethical theory that that judges whether or not something is right by what its consequences are.

INTUITIONALISM: Institutional ethics (a.k.a. organizational ethics) refers to the application of ethics in such institutions as hospitals, professional organization, and corporations. It regards institutions as moral agents with responsibilities and accountability.

EMOTIVISM: the view that moral judgments do not function as statements of fact but rather as expressions of the speaker's or writer's feelings.

DUTY-BASED ETHICS: Duty-based ethics teaches that some acts are right or wrong because of the sorts of things they are, and people have a duty to act accordingly, regardless of the good or bad consequences that may be produced.

VIRTUE ETHICS: Virtue ethics is an approach that treats virtue and character as the primary subjects of ethics, in contrast to other ethical systems that put consequences of voluntary acts, principles or rules of conduct, or obedience to divine authority in the primary role.

SITUATION ETHICS: In Situation Ethics right and wrong depend on the situation. There are no universal moral rules or rights. Each case is unique and deserves a unique solution. Situation Ethics rejects prefabricated decisions and prescriptive rules.

NORMATIVE (PRESCRIPTIVE) ETHICS: Normative Ethics is the study of ethical behavior that investigates questions regarding how one ought to act, in a moral sense. It asks: How should people act?

APPLIED ETHICS: Applied Ethics (a.k.a. Practical Ethics) is the application of ethics to real-world problems, attempting to answer the question of how people should act in specific situations. It asks: How do we take moral knowledge and put it into practice?

META-ETHICS: The study of the meanings of ethical terms, the nature of ethical judgments, and the types of ethical argument. It asks: What does 'right' even mean?

DESCRIPTIVE ETHICS: Descriptive Ethics (a.k.a. comparative ethics) is the study of people's beliefs about morality. It asks: What do people think is right?

ETHICAL DRIFT: Ethical Drift involves an incremental deviation from ethical practice that goes unnoticed by individuals who justify the deviations as acceptable and who believe themselves to be maintaining their ethical boundaries.

ETHICAL FADING: Ethical Fading is a form of self-deception. It occurs when we subconsciously avoid or disguise the moral implications of a decision. It allows us to behave in immoral ways while maintaining the conviction that we are good, moral people.

MORAL DISENGAGEMENT: Moral Disengagement refers to the process where an individual or group of people distances themselves from the normal or usual ethical standards of behavior and then become convinced that new unethical behaviors are justified due often to some perceived extenuating circumstances.

> *Ethics is the difference between what you have a right to do and what is right to do.*
> Potter Stewart.

DEFINITIONS

Respect for the truth is an acquired taste.
Yaz. *Double Team.*

BABELIAN IMPERATIVE: **1.** The act of deceiving through use of a euphemism. **2.** The use of language in deception through obfuscation.

BERNAYS EFFECT: the improper yet successful manipulation of an individual, group or the general public for power, control and authority for financial gain. See: Eddy Bernays, Logical Fallacies, Persuasion Analysis, Propaganda Techniques, and Public Relations.

DELIBERATE DIFFERENCE: setting apart an individual or identifiable group, either expressly or by mute sanction, for different laws, equality, equity, or inactions toward.

DELIBERATE INDIFFERENCE: Deliberate Indifference is the conscious or reckless disregard of the consequences of one's acts or omissions. Deliberate Indifference entails something more than negligence, but is satisfied by something less than acts or omissions for the very purpose of causing harm or with knowledge that harm will result.

DISMISSIVE COGNITION: The psychopathic ability to put aside all Cognitive Dissonance often through Malignant Narcissism, by Dissociation of the humanity of others giving ability in criminality.

DISSOCIATE: **1.** To separate from association or union with another: DISCONNECT, **2.** DISUNITE

DISSOCIATION (Criminal): criminal dissociation involves the separation of humanity of another individual to object status therefore a psychological lessening of the humanity of another that may lead to criminal behavior.

DISSOCIATION: **1a.** The act or process of dissociating: the state of being dissociated **b.** the separation of idea or activity from the mainstream of consciousness or of behavior esp. as a mechanism of ego defense **2.** Psychiatry **a.** A psychological defense mechanism in which specific anxiety producing thoughts, emotions, or physical separations are separated from the rest of the psyche **b.** The separation of a group of mental processes or ideas from the rest of the personality, so that they lead an independent existence.

DISSONANCE: Lack of agreement; *specif*: inconsistency between the beliefs one holds or one's actions and one's beliefs: DISCORD

DISSONANT: **1.** Marked by dissonance: DISCORDANT **2.** INCONGROUS **3.** Harmonically unresolved – dissonantly *adv*

DOMESTICATED VIOLENCE: socialized and/or acculturated use of violence in Transference of Aggression personally and/or interpersonally often detrimental to self and others in ritualistic behavior

DOUBLING: In the psychoanalysis of Robert Lifton, Doubling is the division of the self into two functioning selves, so that a part-self as the entire self.

COLLECTIVE GUILT: guilt of a collective group whether valid or not

MALIGNANT HERO SYNDROME: a person or group of persons who falsely and often maliciously create a crisis then miraculously rush in to solve the problem in a self-glorification

MUNCHAUSEN SYNDROME: also known as factitious disorder is a type of mental disorder in which a person may lie about symptoms, make themselves appear sick, or make themselves purposely unwell with the motive of gaining attention, see: FACTITIOUS DISORDER

MUNCHAUSE SYNDROME BY PROXY: **1.** (Medical, Criminal) Munchausen Syndrome by Proxy is a mental illness and a form of child abuse. The caretaker of a child, most often a mother, either makes up fake symptoms or causes real symptoms or causes real symptoms to make it look like the child is sick. **2.** Munchausen Syndrome by Proxy other than medical is the creation of social stigma onto a person or group of persons with the intent of self-glorify one's difference from the victim person or group of persons.

MUNCHAUSEN COMPLEX: involves Munchausen Syndrome and Munchausen Syndrome by Proxy inclusive to social use often involving a type of self-glorification. see: FACTITIOUS DISORDER

MUNCHAUSEN SYNDROME IN SOCIAL AGENCY: the agency relationship between a person with a primary agency as a parent or care giver relationship as the 'principle,' with a person who accepted secondary agency, usu., a doctor or shaman, that creates an act of abuse

COLLECTIVE MUNCHAUSEN SYNDROME IN SOCIAL AGENCY: the occurrence of Munchausen Syndrome in Social agency with a group of any kind, in part, family, society, or culture

MUNCHAUSEN SYNDROME IN COLLECTIVE TRANSMISSION: **1.** is a delusional transmission of a condition, or simulation of a disease, taken to social or clinical significance, whether to a person or group of persons. **2.** It is the transference of alleged identity to a personal relationship, family, community, society, or culture. **3.** It operates by deliberate transmission, from one generation to subsequent generations of unresolved conflicts, dependencies, and aggressions onto a substitute social body, or social body part, object as wells as heirs

MUNCHAUSEN SYNDROME IN SOCIAL TRANSFERENCE: is the identity transference of the self into a social group that practices forms of Munchausen behavior

MUNCHAUSEN SYNDROME FOR PROFIT: is the fabrication of a problem, or exacerbation of an existing medical condition, often, but not always, from a Specialized Agent as an attorney, health care professional, or other person or interest group, to gain sympathy from others and/or society for financial gain in self-glorification

PASSIVE INITIATION: a person who has someone else act for them

SOCIALIZED STALKING: organized improper social behavior directed toward an individual or group

TRANSGENERATIONAL MUNCHAUSEN SYNDROME: is generational abuse in family and/or social group, community, society, and a step toward acculturation

TRANSFERRED COLLECTIVE GUILT: **1.** The transference of guilt onto an identifiable group from the actions of another or others **2.** Applied collective guilt by substitution through denial, deception, and deferral

TRANSFERRED GUILT: **1.** The transference of guilt onto an identifiable person or group of persons from the actions of another or others. **2.** Applied collective guilt by substitution through denial, deception, and deferral

TRANSFERENCE: The deliberate displacement of one's unresolved conflicts, dependencies, and aggressions onto a substitute object

TRANSFERRED AGGRESSION: **1.** is the situation where you impose your anger on those around you instead of the source of it. **2.** Showing attitudes that are not right for no reason known to them.

TRANSFERRED REPRESENTATION: a transference of identity of an object, a person or objectified body part imparting new meaning that may create an altered meaning or focus of attention whether consciously or unconsciously directed.

Action indeed is the sole medium
of expression for ethics.
Jane Addams

CONDITIONS

*In just about every area of society,
There's nothing more important than ethics.*
Henry Paulson. *U.S. Secretary of the Treasury*

BULLYING: The repetitive, intentional hurting of one person or group by another person or group, where the relationship involves an imbalance of power. Bullying can be physical, verbal or psychological. It can happen face-to-face or online.

GASLIGHTING: Gaslighting is a form of abuse. Similar to Machiavellianism it manipulates. Here a person plants seeds of doubts in an individual or a target group. The objective is to affect memories, perceptions, one's own sanity, in persistent denial, misdirection, contradictions, and lying. The purpose is to destabilize, disorient and delegitimize the victim as well as their belief systems.

Gaslighting is particularly observable in psychiatry and their institutions. Denial of previous abuses to staging of bizarre events is common Defensive Functioning.

Disorienting the victim also includes those around the victim and the organization(s) including all things medical as within the context of a medical Jihad. A victim's ability to resist manipulations relies on the victim trusting their own judgment. Yet, the victim's ability to defend themselves is minimal.

MACHIAVELLIANISM: Machiavellianism in the realm of personality psychology, not the political philosophy of the same name though can be intertwined, is a trait revolving on manipulation, callousness and an indifference to morality. As such there is no Cognitive Dissonance.

Motivation exhibits cold detachment, selfishness, using others as objects to be used as tools to enhance oneself and/or the Self's identified Group through low emotional intelligence and lack of empathy. Machiavellianism, Narcissism (in part genetic) and Psychopathy make up what some psychologists term the Dark Triad.

PSYCHOLOGICAL PROJECTION: Psychological Projection is an *ego defensive mechanism* in denying impulses and attributing them to others. It is accusing others what the person themselves are doing. Similarly, this includes such behaviors as Blame Shifting. What the ego repudiates is split from the Self and then put on another.

That other person may be the person who brought forth the perpetrator's improper behavior, and as a means of retaliation they then attempt to maintain innocence and free themselves of prosecution.

SHARED PSYCHOTIC DISORDER: Shared psychotic disorder (Folie a deux) is a disorder characterized by sharing a delusion among two or more people in a close relationship. The inducer (primary) who has a psychotic disorder with delusions influences another nonpsychotic individual or more (induced, secondary) based of the delusional belief.

PUNITIVE PERSONALITY DISORDER: Punitive Personality Disorder involves a person or group of persons who punish another person, or group of persons, for behavior or innateness. It is steeped in Fear Conditioning in Sadomasochism. It often grows beyond the individual into a social as a form of Mobbing with or without physical violence, and/or cultural transmission of trauma that imprints genetics.

SUGGESTION: Suggestion is an idea or plan put forward for others consideration. It also implies or indicates a certain fact or situation. Suggestion is a psychological process that guides oneself or another's thoughts, feelings, and behaviors.

Beyond simple suggestion, it is often carried with some type of threat. It can also be used as a threat of self-harm if the caretaker does not comply. Punishment for non-compliance may be personal growing to social.

WOUNDED CHILD ARCHETYPE: The Wounded Child is wounded from abuse, neglect or other traumas suffered in childhood. See Carolyn Myss' *Sacred Contracts: Awakening Your Divine Potential*.

The Wounded Child occurs around the ages of 6 to 8. It is when something perceived as wrong happens to the child, often involving the opposite sex or sexual matter, and is also often in front of others. Humiliation is a major factor.

This archetype, as a child and carried into an adult, can often have a deep sense of compassion, understanding and sense the wounds of others because they were wounded themself.

Spiritually, the Wounded Child archetype often acts as an activator for forgiveness. The Shadow may be stuck in self-pity, or blame parents for everything real or perceived. The Shadow may also continually seek out parental figures into adulthood, seeking to fill what was left emotionally unfulfilled in childhood, never allowing them to grow into self-resourcefulness.

These wounds may have been abuse as physical, mental, emotional, sexual, neglect, or trauma. Most often they occur before the individual reaches the age of eight, though this need not always be the case. However, whatever the negative emotional pattern is and whenever it occurs, it is certain that it causes permanent damage that is haunting to them for the rest of their life to some degree.

The individual will have experienced much physical and emotional abuse over the course of their lives. This can have occurred at the hands of one or more people, and can also have happened as one incident or multiple incidents.

Ethics are more important than law.
Michael Moore.

BEHAVIORS

And my rule is: You break it, you bought it.
Yaz. Double Team.

COGNITIVE DISSONANCE: **1.** the state of having inconsistent thoughts, beliefs, or attitudes, especially related to behavioral decisions and attitude change. **2.** The mental stress or discomfort experienced by an individual who holds two or more contradictory beliefs, ideas, or values at the same time, or is confronted by new information that conflicts with existing beliefs, ideas, or values.

CULTURE BOUND SYNDROME: A local pattern of aberrant behavior with troubling experiences. They do not become accepted social behaviors and considered a type of sickness in that society.

CULTURE SPECIFIC SYNDROME: A form of disturbed behavior specific to cultural system. Culture Specific Syndromes are considered normal behavior in that society. They may spread to mother cultures from contact through Cultural Imperialism.

DIFFUSION OF RESPONSIBILITY: (Bystander Effect, Attribution, Darby and Latane) a sociopsychological phenomenon whereby a person is less likely to take responsibility for an action or inaction when others are present. Considered a form of attribution, the individual assumes others are either responsible for taking action or have already done so.

The phenomenon tends to occur in groups of people above a certain critical size and when responsibility is not explicitly assigned.

FEAR CONDITIONING: (Fear by Osmosis) is a behavior in which organisms learn to predict adverse events. It is learning in which adverse stimulus (e.g. electrical shock) is associated with a particular neutral context (e.g. a room) or neutral stimulus (e.g. tone), resulting in the expression of fear responses to the originally neutral stimulus or context. This can be done with paring the neutral stimulus with an adverse stimulus (e.g. shock, loud noise, or unpleasant odor). Eventually. The neutral stimulus alone can elicit the state of fear. In the vocabulary of classical conditioning, the neutral stimulus or context is the "conditional stimulus" (CS) the adverse stimulus is the "unconditional stimulus" US), and the fear is the "conditional response," (CR).

PARALLEL CONSTRUCTION - Legal: Parallel Construction is a subterfuge operation, often but not limited to, used by law enforcement in building a parallel, separate, criminal investigation in order to conceal how and why an investigation began. Evidence laundering, concealing evidence, is when one officer obtains evidence in violation of the 4th Amendment then passes it to another officer who gets it accepted in court. Laundering includes falsifications.

> ***Hold the hand of the child***
> ***that lives in your soul.***
> Paulo Coelho. *The Alchemist.*

COMMUNICATIONS

The world suffers a lot.
Not because of the violence of bad people.
But because of the silence of good people.
Napoleon.

Communication is a basic in how we interact with each other in all ways, including whether ethically or unethically.

Eric Berne, in his book *Games People Play*, discusses communication as it segments into three aspects of our ego. The three ego negotiation elements are the: Parent, Adult, and Child ~ (PAC).

Berne's categories are similar, but not identical, to Freud's psychology as: Parent/ego, Adult/superego, and Child/id. Their actions are:

CHILD: The manner and intent of reaction is the same as it would be for every little boy and girl.

PARENT: To dominate and control children, parents assume certain postures, gestures, vocabulary feelings, etc.

ADULT: This is the mature, autonomous, objective state that appraises situations and states thought processes, perceived problems and conclusions in a non-prejudicial manner.

Jung showed we act by three basic elements:

Persona = Your Mask = Shown to Others
Shadow = You Behind Your Mask = Hidden from All
Ego-Self Relationship = imago Dei = God Within You

Kevin FitzMaurice illustrated that the **nature** of our ego possesses three aspects, with four sections, which act together within us.

Tripartate Nature of the Ego with 4 parts

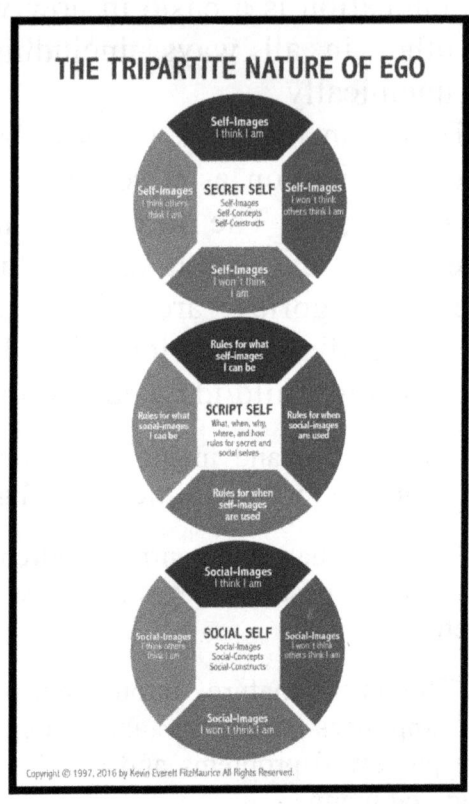

Kevin FitzMaurice illustrated that the **structure** of our ego also possesses three aspects which act together within us.

Tripartite Structure of the Ego

The ego is of thought, not reality

The 3 Thinking Parts of Ego		
GLOBAL THOUGHT	SPECIFIC THOUGHT OF NOW	SPECIFIC THOUGHT OF PAST OR FUTURE
First Thought	Second Thought	Third Thought
Permanent Self	Active Self	Changing Self
Eternal Self	Present Self	Past/Future Self
Judge	Judgment	Judged
Experiencer	Experiencing	Experience
Observer	Performer	Observed
Recorder	Recording	Recorded
Chooser	Actor	Action
Knower	Doer	Be-er
Witness	Cause	Effect
Designer	Programmer	Program
Boss	Worker	Product
Desire	Pursuit	Object
Start	Becoming	End
Actual	Striving	Ideal Future
Defective	Condemning	Damned Past
What-is	Developing	Should-be
Thinker	Thinking	Thought

Copyright © 2016 by Kevin Everett FitzMaurice   https://kevinfitzmaurice.com

Ethics is nothing more than reverence for life.
Albert Schweitzer.

INSTRUCTIONS

Ethics is the difference between what you have a right to do and what is right to do.
Potter Stewart.

This course is meant for you to entertain yourself.

It uses Aphorisms knitted together to inform.

The top is from types of educational thought.

The bottom if from types of the arts as film that imitate life itself.

The top will be more of a Logos statement

The bottom will be more of an Eros statement.

Two examples follow:

Character is higher than intellect.
Ralph Waldo Emerson. *The American Scholar.*

Lessons Learned

When contemplating, think how the Aphorism relates to your own personal and professional relationships, as well as, how all are affected.

Explore the Who, What, When, Where, How, and the hardest of all, the Why. In the beginning you will find you concentrate on each subject tightly.

As you journey and grow, you will discover how subjects interact in our web of existence.

Imagine what you will know tomorrow.
Agent Kay. *Men in Black.*

Lessons Taught

History, fantasy and reality intertwine. Mythic expression is lost. We use the Bible not knowing totem meanings.

Deborah means: "Bee." Her fight was against Bee Goddesses requiring child sacrifice. Newer mythic expression resides mostly in the entertainment industry.

Combining sections aids Archetypical Dimension's psychology where conflict arises from our unconscious id.

If you have integrity, nothing else matters.
If you don't have integrity, nothing else matters.
Alan K, Simpson. *Eyewitness to Power.*

Lessons Learned

You will first think of large concerns of your life's experiences. If you choose to add, add anything that connects with you. Add anecdotes, oddities and other aphorisms.

Concentrate on being light and humorous if possible after sorting possibilities that come to mind.

These will lead you more into the unconscious and associated Patterns of Behavior common to all.

There is no "If."
Nayah. *Devil Girl From Mars.*

Lessons Taught

These Aphorisms will lead you to deeper into the unconscious and will find similarities that lead well into another Aphorism.

Adding your own will lead you to a better understanding of Mythic Expression and the Archetypical Typical dimensions structure from which both, depending on the heart of the individual, Good and Evil emanate.

Thus, through this self-observation you, your family, co-workers and society will greatly benefit

Use the Internet.

You can find Quotes in any subject as well as famous, and not so famous, individuals. One example would be: Abraham Lincoln Quotes.

IMDB is a film industry web page for quotes from most films. You can search by the movie title as well as the film's characters names as: Star Wars with or without adding Yoda quotes.

You may use 25% to 50% of the examples given. You might find some you searched but keep them as yours. The rest will need your work. Do not be afraid to move what you have already done. Play with it. Entertain yourself.

For ease, try setting up a computer file with the worksheet. Then fill in the pages of your self-test under the two sections Lessons Learned and Lesson Taught.

This is not meant to do as a school assignment.
You are given usually 2 Aphorisms per section.
Provide only one of your own per section.
Get relaxed. Do not stress to do it.
Make it a game. Play with it. Digest it.
Get into your Wounded Child.

The child in me is still, and sometimes not so still.
Fred Rogers. *The World According to Mr. Rogers.*

1.

***Educating the mind without educating
The heart is no education at all.***
Aristotle.

Every soul is a battlefield.
Lyman Abbott. *Problems of Life.*

Lessons Learned

***As we learn about each other,
So, we learn about ourselves.***
The Doctor. *Dr. Who.*

***¶Getting to know you,
Getting to know all about you.¶***
Anna. *The King and I.*

Lessons Taught

2.

History is the sum total of all things that could have been avoided.
Konrad Adenauer.

Never use a big word where a diminutive one will suffice.
Anonymous.

Lessons Learned

Ralphus, break a leg.
Master Sardu.
Whose, Master?
Ralphus.
Blood Sucking Freaks.

Lessons Taught

3.

So many come to the sick room thinking of themselves as men of science fighting disease and not as healers with the little knowledge of helping nature to get a sick man well.
Sir Auckland Geddes, M.D., WWI. *The Practitioner.*

Lessons Learned

His therapy was going nowhere.
Hannibal Lecter. *The Silence of the Lambs.*

In the fight for survival there are no rules.
The Doctor. *Dr. Who.*

Lessons Taught

4.

> *When a doctor cannot do good,*
> *he must be kept from doing wrong.*
> Hippocrates. *Epidemics.*

> *It is less a problem to be poor,*
> *than to be dishonest.*
> Junius (Avatar). *Letter to the Editor.*

Lessons Learned

> *Once you give up your integrity,*
> *the rest is a piece of cake.*
> J. R. Ewing. *Dallas.*

> *It's a lot of simple tricks and nonsense.*
> Han Solo. *Star Wars.*

Lessons Taught

5.

*The integrity of men is to be measured
by their conduct, not by their profession.*
Junius (Avatar). Letter to the Editor.

Death takes no bribes.
Benjamin Franklin.

Lessons Learned

*Can you look me in the eye and guarantee me
this is not some sort of flimflam?*
Evelyn. The Mummy.

Where do you keep your dead?
Edgar/Bug. Men in Black.

Lessons Taught

6.

I have always thought the actions of men the best interpreters of their thoughts. Preference to vice to virtue, a manifest wrong judgment.
John Locke. *Essays Concerning Human Understanding.*

The medicine increases the disease.
Virgil. *The Aeneid.*

Lessons Learned

¶Smiling faces, smiling faces tell lies.¶
Norman Whitfield. *The Temptations.*

Oh dear! What an awkward situation.
The Doctor. *Dr. Who.*

Lessons Taught

7.

> ***There are some remedies worse than the disease.***
> Publilius Syrus. *Maxim 283.*

> ***The doctor's visit was without benefit to the patient.***
> Ardant duPicq. *Battle Studies.*

Lessons Learned

> ***Don't listen to me... I never do.***
> The Doctor. *Dr. Who.*

> ***Ah, hard to see the Dark Side is.***
> Yoda. *The Phantom Menace.*

Lessons Taught

8.

> *It is not titles that honor men,*
> *but men that honor titles.*
> Niccolo Machiavelli. *The Prince.*

> **The only fence against the world is a thorough knowledge of it.**
> John Locke. *Some Thoughts Concerning Education.*

Lessons Learned

> *We'll make sure the bodies get dumped a long way from here. We don't want to have any unnecessary questions.*
> Colonel Mekum. *Soldier.*

> *You're all going to die down here.*
> Red Queen. *Resident Evil.*

Lessons Taught

9.

> *The most noble art of medicine*
> *is knowing when to do nothing.*
> Mark Twain.

> *You must be the change you wish*
> *to see in the world.*
> Anonymous. *Misattributed to Ghandi.*

Lessons Learned

_____
_____
_____
_____

> *It's not just the doctor-patient ethics thing at all.*
> Anthony Soprano. *The Sopranos.*

> *So, you lie to yourself to be happy.*
> Teddy. *Memento.*

Lessons Taught

_____
_____
_____
_____

10.

A doctor's reputation is made by the number of eminent men who die under his care.
George Bernard Shaw. *George Bernard Shaw: His Life and Personality.* 1942.

Even paranoids have real enemies.
Delmore Schwartz.

Lessons Learned

It's not paranoia. The embedding's very subtle.
David Levinson. *Independence Day.*

Paranoia is ultimate awareness.
Robert Durant. *Darkman II.*

Lessons Taught

11.

A man without ethics is a wild beast loosed upon this world.
Manly P. Hall. *Attributed.*

It is only in literature that coincidences seem unnatural.
Robert Wilson Lynd.

Lessons Learned

To be a psychiatrist in the country is to be an expert of paranoia, whether you're meant to be or not.
Bukhanovsky. *Citizen X.*

*It's nothing personal.
But in an hour, maybe two, you'll be dead.*
Alice. *Resident Evil: Apocalypse.*

Lessons Taught

12.

Aggression unchallenged is aggression unleashed.
Phaedrus.

A covenant not to defend myself from force, by force, is void.
Thomas Hobbes. *Leviathan.*

Lessons Learned

*People who have no hope are easy to control.
And whoever has the control has the power.*
G'mork. *The NeverEnding Story.*

I executed everyone.
Ada Wong. *Resident Evil: Retribution.*

Lessons Taught

13.

Every life is a march from innocence, through temptation, to virtue or vice. ... Do not think you can fight corruption without while you let corruption fester within.
Lyman Abbott. Problems of Life.

Lessons Learned

_____
_____
_____

Where there is will, there is a weapon.
Yuri. Lord of War.

He's much too sophisticated for the standard tests.
Dr. Fredrick Chilton. The Silence of the Lambs.

Lessons Taught

_____
_____
_____

14.

Egotism is that special something which enables a man who's in a rut think he is in a groove.
Anonymous.

Evils draw men together.
Aristotle. *Rhetoric.*

Lessons Learned

What is it about earth people that makes them think a futile gesture is a noble one?
Thurlough. *Dr. Who.*

*I am the beginning. The end.
The one who is many.*
Borg Queen. *Star Trek: First Contact.*

Lessons Taught

15.

People inflict pain on others in the selfish pursuit of their happiness or satisfaction.
Dalai Lama. *Nobel Peace Prize Acceptance Speech.*

He who does not punish evil, commands it to be done.
Leonardo da Vinci.

Lessons Learned

*It was the duty of those teams to segregate the prisoners of war who were candidates for execution. ...
And to report to the office of the Gestapo.*
K. Lindeau. *Nuremberg Trial.*

Lessons Taught

16.

Any action for which there is no logical explanation will be "Company Policy."
Second Law of the Corporation.

Quality assurance doesn't.
Robertson's Law.

Lessons Learned

Sloppiness breeds inefficiency.
Major Powers. *Heartbreak Ridge.*

I helped the strangers conduct their experiments. I have betrayed my own kind.
Dr. Schreber. *Dark City.*

Lessons Taught

17.

Genocide requires both a specific victim group and certain relationships to that group.
Robert Lifton. *The Nazi Doctors.*

Let the punishment match the offense.
Cicero. *De Liguibus.*

Lessons Learned

He was getting away with murder because no one was firing back.
Narrator. *Target: Pearl Harbor.*

The Red Queen attempted to kill everyone.
Alice. *Resident Evil: Retribution.*

Lessons Taught

18.

The morality of killing is not something with which the professional soldier is usually not thought to trouble himself with.
Aristotle.

Evil is fittest to consort with evil.
Livy. *Annales.*

Lessons Learned

Tell me, was it public relations you did for the gestapo or community relations.
Burke. *The Exorcist.*

You better find a way to make it easy, soldier, or I'm going to start pushing buttons.
Lily Sloane. *Star Trek: First Contact.*

Lessons Taught

19.

There is no emotional reservoir to relate to vulnerability, pain and fear of the victim.
Aristotle.

Let the welfare of the people be the ultimate law.
Cicero.

Lessons Learned

It is important that we distinguish between someone who has had a bad day that ends in a temper tantrum, and someone whose failure to resist aggressive impulses in serious destructive acts.
Trina Gavin. *Jade.*

Lessons Taught

20.

I've destroyed my passions, rather like a violent man who, finding he can't control his horse, kills it.
Nicolas Chamfort. *Maxims of Pensee, #325.*

An evil life is a kind of death.
Ovid.

Lessons Learned

Nice guys are fine, you have to have somebody to take advantage of.
Porter. *Payback.*

You're really quite charming when you're not killing people.
Nika. *Hitman.*

Lessons Taught

21.

***Common sense is in medicine
is the master workman.***
Peter Latham. *Collected Works.*

***They have not the sure direction
of a weapon well in hand.***
Ardant duPicq. *Battle Studies.*

Lessons Learned

You have no idea the power you try to control.
Dr. Brodeus. *Miss Ever's Boys.*

Violence and technology – not good bedfellows.
Eddie Carr. *Lost World: Jurassic Park.*

Lessons Taught

22.

Whoever merely tastes of his error, will keep house with it for a long time. ... but whoever drains it completely will have to get to know it.
Goethe. *Apprenticeship.*

Lessons Learned

I'm Bad Ash and you're Good Ash.
Evil Ash. *Army of Darkness.*

They are blind to the darkness within themselves.
Trina Gavin. *Jade.*

Lessons Taught

23.

A man always has two reasons for what he does –
a good one, and a real one.
J.P. Morgan. Attributed in: *Owen Wister: "Roosevelt: The Story of a Friendship."*

I have a plan.
Bert. *Tremors.*

Lessons Learned

You have a Harvard education,
make something up!
Marlene. *Dr. Who.*

A man can convince anyone he's somebody else,
but never himself.
Verbal. *The Usual Suspects.*

Lessons Taught

24.

Having lots of ideas doesn't mean you're clever, any more than having lots of soldiers means you're a good general.
Nicolas Chamfort. *Reflections*

Cleverness is not wisdom.
Euripides. *Bacchae I: 395.*

Lessons Learned

Battlefield doctors decide who lives and who dies.
Johns.
They kept calling it murder when I did it.
Riddick.
Pitch Black.

Must I hack down a whole family tree of demons?
Beowulf. *Beowulf.*

Lessons Taught

25.

Educating the mind without educating
The heart is no education at all.
Aristotle.

Every soul is a battlefield.
Lyman Abbott. *Problems of Life.*

Lessons Learned

Especially important is the warning to avoid conversations with the demon. We may ask what is relevant but anything else is dangerous.
He is a Liar.
Father Merrin. *The Exorcist.*

Lessons Taught

26.

The mastery of nature is vainly believed to be an adequate substitute for self-mastery.
Reinhold Niebuhr. *Moral Man and Immoral Society.*

   False ambition serves the neck.
   Egyptian Proverb.

Lessons Learned

The duality of man, the Jungian thing, Sir!
Joker. *Full Metal Jacket.*

If it bleeds, we can kill it.
Dutch. *Predator.*

Lessons Taught

27.

To thy death art thou sped;
Until God's word be said.
In the white lily bloom,
Brave Boy is thy tomb.
The Brothers Grimm.

All things can corrupt perverse minds.
Ovid.

Lessons Learned

Whatever hurts you makes you stronger.
Elizabeth Campbell. *The General's Daughter.*

¶Hear them scream for shelter,
from the world they never found.¶
Grand Funk Railroad. *I Can Feel Him in the Morning.*

Lessons Taught

28.

The history of medicine is a story of amazing foolishness and amazing intelligence.
Jerome Tarshis.
Claude Bernard: Father Experimental Medicine.

Bad conduct soils the finest ornament more than filth.
Plautus.

Lessons Learned

*Some of the most successful relationships are based on lies and deceit.
Since that's where they usually wind up anyway, that's a logical place to start.*
Yuri. *Lord of War.*

Dirt cleans off a lot easier than blood.
Maximus. *Gladiator.*

Lessons Taught

29.

> *Once he has killed, that taboo was gone.*
> *He realized he could do it, enjoy it,*
> *and get away with it.*
> John Douglas and Mark Olshaker. *Mind Hunter.*

> *We can learn even from our enemies.*
> Ovid.

Lessons Learned

> *That, sir, is protracted war.*
> The Doctor. *Dr. Who.*

> *We can be as different as we wanna be,*
> *but you can't kill people.*
> Anna. *The King and I.*

Lessons Taught

30.

Force shites on reason's back.
Benjamin Franklin. *Poor Richard's Almanack.*

*Eminence without merit earns
deference without esteem.*
Nicolas Chamfort. *Maxims and Pensees, c. 1805.*

Lessons Learned

*It's hells plan to keep the new recruits
confused hoping to discourage the warriors
of any personal attack.*
The Doctor. *Dr. Who.*

You get what you settle for.
Louise. *Thelma and Louise.*

Lessons Taught

31.

You may deceive all the people part of the time and part of the people all of the time but not all the people all the time.
Abraham Lincoln.
Speech, Clinton Illinois, 02 September 1858.

Lessons Learned

Like Alice, I try to believe three impossible things before breakfast.
The Doctor. *Dr. Who.*

You'll never know when someone's going to come along with a sadistic choice.
Green Goblin. *Spiderman.*

Lessons Taught

32.

*A tyrant claims freedom to kill,
and yet keep it for himself.*
Rabindranth Tagore.
The English Writings of Rabindranth Tagore Poems.

A bad heart, bad designs.
Terence. *Andria.*

Lessons Learned

Pathetic earthlings. Hurling your bodies out into the void, without the slightest inkling of who or what is out there.
Ming the Merciless. *Flash Gordon.*

I may be bad, but I feel good.
Sheila. *Army of Darkness.*

Lessons Taught

33.

Nearly all men can stand adversity, but if you want to test a man's character, give him power.
Abraham Lincoln. *Questionable Attribution.*

The measure of a man is what he does with power.
Pitticus.

Lessons Learned

The Dark Side has clouded their vision.
Count Dooku. *Attack of the Clones.*

I became different. Powerful. Unstoppable. As I got stronger, the human race got weaker.
Alice. *Resident Evil: Retribution.*

Lessons Taught

34.

*Sometimes we choose to suffer alone;
Sometimes we choose to make others
suffer with us.*
M.

*No one is truly literate who cannot
read his own heart.*
Eric Hoffer. *The Passionate State of Mind.*

Lessons Learned

Suffering is the coin of the realm.
Pinhead. *Hellraiser IV: Bloodline.*

*Most women have a few barriers around their
heart, But Eva has an electrified fence
with rabid pit bulls.*
Ray. *Deliver us from Eva.*

Lessons Taught

35.

Pain is deeper than all thought.
Elbert Hubbard. *Selected Writings. 1922.*

Violence begets fear.
Jay Carney. *White House Press Brief, 1999.*

Lessons Learned

What she means is she prefers the senseless pain we inflict on each other to the pain we would otherwise inflict on ourselves.
Jessup. *Altered States.*

His is a tale of sorrow.
Sobotai the Mongol. *Conan.*

Lessons Taught

36.

People who bite the hand that feeds them usually lick the boot that kicks them.
Eric Hoffer. *Attributed.*

Who profits by a sin has done the sin.
Seneca the Younger.

Lessons Learned

Killing you and what you represent is a statement.
Mickey Mallory. *Natural Born Killers.*

We should not have made this bargain.
Nute Gunray. *Star Wars: The Phantom Menace.*

Lessons Taught

37.

> *None so deaf as those who will not hear.*
> English Proverb.

> *We lie loudest when we lie to ourselves.*
> Eric Hoffer.
> The Passionate State of Mind, and Other Aphorisms.

Lessons Learned

> *Your scientists were so preoccupied with whether or no they could, they didn't stop to think if they should.*
> Dr. Malcom. *Jurassic Park.*

> *You sharpen the human appetite to the point of where it can split atoms with its desire.*
> John Milton. *Devil's Advocate.*

Lessons Taught

38.

There is always the mad impatience for results, without considering the means.
Ardant duPicq. *Battle Studies.*

Of war men ask the outcome, not the cause.
Seneca the Younger.

Lessons Learned

I'm Finn of Frisia and my name shall be remembered forever!
Finn.
Only if you kill me. Otherwise, you are nothing.
Beowulf.
Beowulf.

You've operated behind the scenes to suborn the trust of a man.
Joe. *Meet Joe Black.*

Lessons Taught

39.

> *When argument fails, try abuse.*
> Anonymous.

> *It is in your moments of decision
> that your destiny is shaped.*
> Anthony Robbins.

Lessons Learned

> *Behold, I send you out as sheep amidst the wolves.*
> Alice Lomax. *Devil's Advocate.*

> *It looks like a type of disorder that you rarely see
> anymore, except in primitive cultures.*
> Dr. Barringer. *The Exorcist.*

Lessons Taught

40.

The human race has a long history of hurting the ones we love – or should love.
John Douglas and Mark Olshaker. *Mind Hunter.*

All savageness is a sign of weakness.
Seneca the Younger.

Lessons Learned

Plague, famine. War. Morality doesn't even enter into it.
Deacon Frost. *Blade.*

The people who commit these acts are no longer able to control their urges.
Trina Gavin. *Jade.*

Lessons Taught

41.

Pain is such an uncomfortable feeling that even a tiny amount of it is enough to ruin every enjoyment.
Will Rogers.

Both the petal and the thorn belong to the rose.
M.

Lessons Learned

Pain, suffering, death I feel. Something terrible has happened.
Yoda. *Attack of the Clones.*

This wasn't the deal! This wasn't the deal!
White Rabbit. *Manhunter.*

Lessons Taught

42.

No human being who is moved to action through wrong motivations or misuses the privileges of his times, can be regarded as educated, regardless of the amount of formal schooling he has received.
Manly P. Hall. *The Secret Destiny of America.*

Lessons Learned

Is it true before you took Holy Orders you were a used car salesman?
Father Burke. *Trouble Along the Way.*

I don't want to believe it but, there is no man, Giffy. Only that moon.
Sally Owens. *Practical Magic.*

Lessons Taught

43.

*In rivers of bad government,
the lightest things swim at the top.*
Benjamin Franklin.

He who spares the wicked injures the good.
Seneca. *Attributed.*

Lessons Learned

I know the misery they cause. The destruction.
The Doctor. *Dr. Who.*

Eva's sisters gave her a cross with Jesus on it for her birthday, the next day Jesus was gone.
Darrell. *Deliver Us from Eva.*

Lessons Taught

44.

Practice proves more than theory.
Abraham Lincoln. *Annual Message to Congress, 1862.*

If virtue precedes us every step will be safe.
Seneca. *Attributed.*

Lessons Learned

He plans in obsessive detail what props he'll bring and what knots he'll tie.
Helen Hudson. *Copycat.*

You are what you do.
A man is defined by his actions.
Kuato. *Total Recall.*

Lessons Taught

45.

The first killer I ever studied had put bandages over the wounds of the people he stabbed once they were dead.
Robert Ressler. *I Have Lived in the Monster.*

Every guilty man is his own hangman.
Seneca the Elder.

Lessons Learned

Just go forward in all your beliefs and prove to me that I am not mistaken in mine.
The Doctor. *Dr. Who.*

*They say you have a monster here.
They say your land is cursed.*
Beowulf. *Beowulf.*

Lessons Taught

46.

*Nations are born of those who love the truth,
and are buried when they forget it.*
Manly P. Hall. *Ark of the Covenant.*

Nations die first in big cities.
Austin O'Malley.

Lessons Learned

*The future, Madame, is something we should have
started on a long time ago.*
Doctor Genessier. *Eyes Without a Face.*

He does not know why the sacrifice is demanded.
Bukhanovsky. *Citizen X.*

Lessons Taught

47.

I believe that this neglected, wounded inner child of the past is the major source of human misery.
John Bradshaw. *Homecoming.*

The sun also shines on the wicked.
Seneca the Elder.

Lessons Learned

I will buy his secret in a bounty of pain.
Pinhead. *Hellraiser IV: Bloodline.*

***¶There will be lies never erased.
Along with the lives never replaced.¶***
Catie Curtis. *Same Dream.*

Lessons Taught

48.

Nothing fixes a thing as intensely in the memory as the wish to forget it.
Michael D. Montaigne. Essais.

Little by little one walks far.
Peruvian Proverb.

Lessons Learned

*¶The warship had landed and I came ashore,
The fighting was over for me evermore.
For I had been wounded, they left me for dead.¶*
Ernest Tubb. *Missing in Action.*

Lessons Taught

49.

The existence of forgetting has never been proved; we only know that some things do not come to our mind when we want them to.
Nietzsche.

Clear conscious never fears midnight knocking.
Chinese Proverb.

Lessons Learned

You think you do not remember but your blood knows, let it remind you.
Princess Angelique. *Hellraiser: Bloodline.*

Forget about it. I do think that Aunt Martha and I have a right to our own little secrets.
Abby. *Arsenic and Old Lace.*

Lessons Taught

50.

***We can only know as adults
what we feel as children.***
Leslie Fielder.
Huckleberry Finn: First in the Eden of Childhood.

***Men are of no importance.
What counts is who commands.***
Charles de Gaulle. *New Yor Times, 1965.*

Lessons Learned

***They do violence in their grandmother's
neighborhoods.***
The Doctor. *Dr. Who.*

***You mean we're all going to die 'cause you
screwed up on the math?***
Pantucci. *Deep Rising.*

Lessons Taught

51.

*We do not see nature with our eyes,
but with our understandings and our hearts.*
Hazlitt. *Thoughts on Taste.*

*All leaders strive to turn
their followers into children.*
Eric Hoffer.

Lessons Learned

¶I landed in this country. With one year of life to give, my only friend a weapon. And my only prayer, to live. I walked away from freedom, The life that I had known.¶
Chuck Rosenberg. *Boonie Rat.*

Lessons Taught

52.

Though the physical attack was over, now enters a new phase. It is inflicted on the victim's soul.
Rape Expert. *Sexual Violence: Our War Against Rape.*

Depression is frozen anger.
David Seamand.

Lessons Learned

There is nothing like an amputated spirit. There is not a prosthetic device for that.
Frank Slade. *Scent of a Woman.*

The sword is no match for demonic magic.
Beowulf. *Beowulf.*

Lessons Taught

53.

> *Science is organized knowledge.*
> *Wisdom is organized life.*
> Immanuel Kant. *Critique of Pure Reason.*

> *Any excuse will serve a tyrant.*
> Aesop.

Lessons Learned

> *Keep it confused, feed it with useless information.*
> The Doctor. *Dr. Who.*

> *She's only trying to deceive us... deceive us... she'll say anything to stop us shutting down.*
> Kaplan. *Resident Evil.*

Lessons Taught

54.

In respect of civil rights, all citizens are equal before the law. The humblest is the peer of the most powerful.
John Marshall Harlan. *U.S. Supreme Court, 1898.*

History is philosophy learned from example.
Thucydides.

Lessons Learned

God created dinosaurs. God destroys dinosaurs. God creates man. Man creates dinosaurs.
The Malcom.
Dinosaurs eat man. Woman inherits the earth.
Dr. Sattler.
Jurassic Park.

Lessons Taught

55.

> *All classes are criminal today. We live in an age of equality.*
> Joe Orton. *Funeral Games.*

> *How dreadful it is when the right judge judges wrong.*
> Sophocles. *Sentry, 'Antigone.'*

Lessons Learned

> *Think we better decide what brings out the best in humankind, and what brings out the worst, because it's either the stars or the jungle*
> Morgan. *The Creature Walks Among Us.*

Lessons Taught

56.

If one does not know to which port one is sailing, no wind is favorable.
Seneca the Younger. *Epistulae morales ad Luculium.*

Nice guys finish last, but we get to sleep in.
Evan Davis.

Lessons Learned

They say most of your brain shuts down during cryo- sleep. All but the primitive side, the animal side.
Riddick. *Pitch Black.*

You simply never understand the true meaning of sacrifice.
May Morrison. *The Wickerman.*

Lessons Taught

57.

Civilization has made man, if not always more bloodthirsty, at least more viciously, more horribly bloodthirsty.
Fyodor Dostoyevsky. *The Insulted and the Injured.*

Eagles fly alone.
English Proverb.

Lessons Learned

I could see the faces of the cult who did this to me, and the dip responsible. All members of the Deadly Viper Assassination Squad.
The Doctor. *Dr. Who.*

The wolf moves among sheep.
Riddick. *The Chronicles of Riddick.*

Lessons Taught

58.

For the original act which the body politic is formed and united does not determine what it shall do to preserve itself.
Jean-Jacque Rousseau. *The Social Contract.*

Good leading makes good following.
Dutch Proverb.

Lessons Learned

I think the point is to make us despair. To see ourselves as... animal and ugly. To see us reject the possibility that God could love us.
Father Merrin. *The Exorcist.*

Lessons Taught

59.

***When the President does it,
that means it is not illegal.***
Richard Nixon. 1977.

The judge is condemned when the criminal is absolved.
Publilius Syrus. *Senteniae.*

Lessons Learned

Before he arrived, the whole place was beginning to look like a reptile house.
Lord James D'Ampton. *Lair of the White Worm.*

Free will. I only see the stage. You pull your own strings.
John Milton. *Devil's Advocate.*

Lessons Taught

60.

Rights are invariably abridged as despotism increases.
Tacitus. *The Annals, Book III.*

Bureaucracy is a giant mechanism run by pigmies.
Honore De Balzac.

Lessons Learned

It's: buy futures, sell futures, when there are no futures.
John Milton. *Devil's Advocate.*

Can man control his destiny?
Can he shape the way of things to come?
George. *The Time Machine.*

Lessons Taught

61.

No written law has ever been more binding than unwritten custom supported by popular opinion.
Carrie Chapman Catt. *Suffragette speech, 1900.*

No grass grows on the battlefield.
Polish Proverb.

Lessons Learned

―――――――――――――――――
―――――――――――――――――
―――――――――――――――――

It isn't a trial; it's a coroner's inquest – a much simpler procedure.
William Hallack. *Thinner.*

They dissociate themselves from their own actions, and often experience a hysterical blindness.
Trina Gavin. *Jade.*

Lessons Taught

―――――――――――――――――
―――――――――――――――――
―――――――――――――――――

62.

A cynic is a man who when he smells flowers looks for the coffin.
H. L. Mencken.

Well done is better than well said.
Benjamin Franklin. *Attributed.*

Lessons Learned

We'll there's nothing like avoiding a little manslaughter charge to turn a man's life around.
Kirk. *Thinner.*

If your strength and heart was as strong and fierce as your words Grendel would not feel free to murder.
Beowulf. *Beowulf.*

Lessons Taught

63.

***Not everything that can be counted counts.
And not everything that counts can be counted.***
William Bruce Cameron.
Wrongly Attributed to Albert Einstein.

He who angers you, controls you.
Anonymous.

Lessons Learned

***I'm a Mog: half man, half dog.
I'm my own best friend.***
Barf. *Spaceballs.*

What are you talking about? I am half the man you are.
Jay. *Men in Black.*

Lessons Taught

64.

*In giving rights to others which belong to them,
We give rights to ourselves and to our country.*
John F. Kennedy.
Recorded: White House, 20 September 1962.

You can't shake hands with a clenched fist.
Indira Ghandi.

Lessons Learned

*There can be no understanding between the hand
and the brain unless the heart acts as mediator.*
Maria. *Metropolis.*

I must penetrate the heart of his secret.
Dr. Caligari. *Dos Cabinet des Dr. Caligari.*

Lessons Taught

65.

Understanding the spirit of our institutions to aim at the elevation of men. I am opposed to whatever tends to degrade them.
Abraham Lincoln
Letter to Dr. Theodore Canisius, 17 May 1859

Cultural Convention Usurps the Rule of Law.
M.

Lessons Learned

¶Come on all you strong young men; Uncle Sam needs your help again; He's got himself in a terrible jam; way down yonder in Vietnam; So put down your books and pick up a gun; we're gonna have a whole lot of fun.¶
Joe McDonald. *Fixin to Die Rag.*

Lessons Taught

66.

Justice is open to everybody in the same way as the Ritz Hotel.
Judge Sturgess. *22 July 1928.*

Justice too long delayed is justice denied.
Lyman Abbott. *Problems of Life.*

Lessons Learned

***Oh, we have 12 vacancies.
12 cabins, 12 vacancies.***
Norman Bates. *Psycho.*

Without their death, their pain, without the sacrifice, we would be nothing.
Tyler Durden. *Fight Club.*

Lessons Taught

67.

One is usually afraid of things which seem to be overpowering.
Carl Jung. *Psychology and Religion.*

Rights are meaningless unless enforced
John Owen Haley. *Authority Without Power.*

Lessons Learned

Do you hear that? That is the sound of a thousand terrible things headed this way.
Qui-Gon Jinn. *The Phantom Menace.*

Some animals are more equal than others.
Benjamin. *Animal Farm.*

Lessons Taught

68.

If there were indeed two killers, one would be the dominate, aggressive, and organized leader, and the other the more passive and possibly disorganized follower.
Robert Ressler. *I Have Lived in the Monster.*

Lessons Learned

I was forging documents before your parents were born.
Arthur. *Apt Pupil.*

Once again, we find ourselves fighting for our lives.
Alice. *Resident Evil: Retribution.*

Lessons Taught

69.

Society is produced by our wants and government by our wickedness.
Thomas Paine. *Common Sense.*

Nobody can acquire honor by doing what is wrong.
Thomas Jefferson.

Lessons Learned

*So long as the paperwork is clean,
You boys can do as you like out there.*
MacAfee. *Mad Max.*

He was killed by some sort of monster, I saw it.
Steve. *The Blob.*

Lessons Taught

70.

To move in a genocidal direction, that cure must be total. It becomes an all-or-nothing matter, equally absolute in its claims to truth and in its rejection of alternate claims.
Robert Lifton. *The Nazi Doctors*.

Lessons Learned

Peace isn't merely the absence of conflict, but the presence of justice.
President James Marshall. *Air Force One*.

Keep a memory of me, not as a king or a hero; but as a man: fallible and flawed.
Beowulf. *Beowulf*.

Lessons Taught

71.

Wrong must not win by technicalities.
Aeschylus. *The Oresteia.*

We learn from history that we do not learn from history.
Hegel.

Lessons Learned

In the world of advertising there is no such thing as a lie. There is only expedient exaggeration.
Thornhill. *North by Northwest.*

They have a sophisticated communication system.
Voice. *Empire of the Ants.*

Lessons Taught

72.

The Rule of Law can be wiped out in one misguided, however well-intentional generation.
William T. Gossett.
President American Bar Association, 1969.

The Register of Knowledge of Fact is called History.
Hobbes.

Lessons Learned

Here's to plain speaking and clear understanding.
Gutman. *The Maltese Falcon.*

Seasons came and went, and we waited. The years passed, we grew old, but we still waited.
Jessie. *Animal Farm.*

Lessons Taught

73.

Many killers, when arrested, express surprise that society should care so much about their victim, for whom the killers have only contempt.
Robert Ressler. *I Have Lived in the Monster.*

Lessons Learned

The Geneva Convention is void here. Amnesty International doesn't know we exist.
Walton. *Face Off.*

What do you know of me, demon?
Beowulf. *Beowulf.*

Lessons Taught

74.

Whereas each man claims his freedom as a matter of right, the freedom he accords to other men is a matter of toleration.
Walter Lippmann. *The Indispensable Opposition, 1939.*

True creativity often starts when language ends.
Koestler.

Lessons Learned

I'm not going to waste my time arguing with a man who is lining up to be a hot lunch.
Hooper. *Jaws.*

The thing I admire most about you... is your ability to suffer in silence. Don't ever change.
Yorke. *Tevil Heritage.*

Lessons Taught

75.

Whenever Law ends, Tyranny begins.
John Locke.
Book II: Two Treatises on Government,

All bad precedents begin as justifiable measures.
Caius Julias Caesar. *Sullust's Conspiracy of Catiline.*

Lessons Learned

He's not being tried. He's being disposed of.
Learned Judge. *Planet of the Apes.*

It just sounds to me like you need to unplug, man.
Choi. *The Matrix.*

Lessons Taught

76.

*Educating the mind without educating
The heart is no education at all.*
Aristotle.

Every soul is a battlefield.
Lyman Abbott. *Problems of Life.*

Lessons Learned

We decided to make it a female so it would be more docile and controllable.
Xavier Fitch.
You guys don't get out much.
Preston Lennox.
Species.

Lessons Taught

77.

Of course, everything has been said that needs to be said. But since no one was listening it has to be said again.
Anonymous.

A lie told often enough becomes the truth.
V. I. Lenin.

Lessons Learned

Resistance is futile. Supreme Dalek. *Dr. Who. Star Trek films. Godzilla: Final Wars. Vampire Hunter D., Bloodlust.*

They can't tell the truth, even to themselves.
Commoner. *Rashomon.*

Lessons Taught

78.

Idealism increases in direct proportion to one's distance from the problem.
John Glasworthy.

The rotten apple spoils the companion.
Benjamin Franklin.

Lessons Learned

You are accused of killing over a thousand civilians. How do you plead?
Rebel Leader
Guilty, but with explanation.
Government Soldier.
Bananas.

Lessons Taught

79.

We are responsible for the world in which we find ourselves, if only because we are the only sentient force which can change it.
James Baldwin. No Name in the Street, 1972.

The first principle is that you must not fool yourself.
Feynman.

Lessons Learned

Your Honor. ... We fight for honor, not gold.
Beowulf.
And the nightmare renews anew? No.
I visited this horror upon my kingdom.
I must be the one to finish her.
Wealthow.
Beowulf.

Lessons Taught

80.

> *An America with two legal standards is*
> *An America with no legal standards.*
> Jim Traficante.

> *Where knowledge is a duty, ignorance is a crime.*
> Thomas Paine.

Lessons Learned

> *I ask for so little. Let me just rule you.*
> Goblin King Jareth. *Labyrinth.*

> *Only stupid earth brains like yours would have been fooled.*
> Cyberman. *Dr. Who.*

Lessons Taught

81.

In the case of every horrible crime since the beginning of civilization, there is always that searing, fundamental question: What kind of person could have done such a thing.
John Douglas and Mark Olshaker. *Mind Hunter.*

Lessons Learned

Watch out for sea monsters. I'm sure your imagination must be teeming with them.
Unferth. *Beowulf.*

It is clear to me the Republic no longer functions.
Queen Amidala. *The Phantom Menace.*

Lessons Taught

82.

Humiliate the reason and distort the soul.
Fyodor Dostoyevsky. *The Idiot.*

The seeking of one thing will find another.
Irish Proverb.

Lessons Learned

They didn't tell me; do you think they're going to tell me about the God damned spin-off.
Tom Sanders. *Disclosure.*

You're the Rigger, I'm the trigger…. Enjoy.
Ray. *The Specialist.*

Lessons Taught

83.

How many ages hence shall our lofty scene be acted over in states unborn and accents yet unknown.
Cassius. *Julius Caesar.*

The elegance of honesty needs no adornment.
Merry Browne.

Lessons Learned

I like to kill them softly, from a distance. Not close enough for feelings.
Cogan. *Killing Them Softly.*

The contract was vague on certain points.
Bilbo Baggins. *The Hobbit.*

Lessons Taught

84.

We have relived our own pain by inflicting it on others.
Philip Caputo. *A Rumor of War.*

She does not know what she sacrifices…. She must be obeyed.
Emma Jung. *Animus and Anima.*

Lessons Learned

The hymn and praise of the few became the curse of the many.
The Doctor. *Dr. Who.*

Don't you think every woman wants a man who will die for her.
Maiden. *Downward Angel.*

Lessons Taught

85.

After a while you learn the subtle difference between holding a hand and chaining the human soul.
Anonymous.

Some children do not survive adult entertainment.
M.

Lessons Learned

Should choose to test my resolve in this matter, you will be facing a finality beyond your comprehension, and you will not be counting days, or months, or years.
Joe Black. *Meet Joe Black.*

Lessons Taught

86.

> *Most of these guys have no burn out point.*
> John Douglas and Mark Olshaker. *Mind Hunter.*

> *The place where optimism flourishes most is the lunatic asylum.*
> Havelock Ellis.

Lessons Learned

> *Why do you attack us?* Zarkov.
> *Why not?* Ming the Merciless.
> *Flash Gordon.*

> *Enter here and die.*
> Widow of the Web. *Krull.*

Lessons Taught

87.

It's a poor rule that won't work both ways.
Frederick Douglas. *On Mexico, 1849.*

In order to become the master, the politician poses as a servant.
Charles De Gaulle.

Lessons Learned

Be my victim. My altar awaits your sacrifice.
Candyman. *Candyman 3.*

You have learned to bury your guilt with anger.
Ducard. *Batman Begins.*

Lessons Taught

88.

An idea to be suggestive, must come to an individual with the force of revelation.
William James. *The Varieties of Religious Experience.*

To know and not to do, is not to know.
Chinese Proverb.

Lessons Learned

The force will have a strong influence on the weak-minded.
Ben Obi-Wan Kenobi. *Star Wars.*

So those mindless beasts of the subconscious had access to a machine that could never be shut down.
Adams. *Forbidden Planet.*

Lessons Taught

89.

Violent offenders usually begin where they feel most comfortable and at home.
John Dougles and Mark Olshaker. *Journey into Darkness.*

Rotten wood cannot be carved.
Chinese Proverb,

Lessons Learned

You sit around here and you spin your little webs and you think the whole world revolves around you.
George Bailey. *It's a Wonderful Life.*

So he assumes the identity of his alter-ego.
Stanley. *Smokin' Aces.*

Lessons Taught

90.

The law is the last resort of human wisdom acting upon human experience for the benefit of the public.
Samuel Johnson. *It's a Wonderful Life.*

To see the right and not do it is cowardice.
Confucious.

Lessons Learned

When you understand the nature of the thing, you know what is capable of.
Blade. *Blade.*

Don't clutter up a clever scheme with morality.
Bowen. *DragonHeart.*

Lessons Taught

91.

Imagination is the eye of the soul.
Joubert.

Imagination is more important than knowledge.
Albert Einstein.

Lessons Learned

No dream is too extreme.
Pinocchio. *Pinocchio.*

They just love the hidden memories of what they've done, which is almost worse.
Avalyn. *Mysterious Skin.*

Lessons Taught

92.

Serial killers play a most dangerous game. The more we understand the way they play, the more we can stack the odds against them.
John Douglas and Mark Olshaker. *Mind Hunter.*

In shallow waters, shrimps make fools of dragons.
Chinese Proverb.

Lessons Learned

There can only be One.
Kurgan. *Highlander.*

¶One is a lonely number.¶
Three Dog Night. *One is the Loneliest Number.*

Lessons Taught

93.

What you do speaks so loud that I cannot hear what you say. What you are thunders so that I cannot hear what you say to the contrary.
Ralph Waldo Emerson. *Letters and Social Aims.*

Lessons Learned

First of all, I shall say that the arguments by the counsel for the defense were sound. Mere Sound.
Adam Bonner. *Adam's Rib.*

You were never meant to enter.
Guardian of the Gate. *The Trial.*

Lessons Taught

94.

Often the less there is to justify a traditional custom, the harder it is to get rid of it.
Mark Twain. *The Adventures of Tom Sawyers.*

In a broken nest there are few whole eggs.
Chinese Proverb.

Lessons Learned

Where would Tina Turner be right now if she rolled over and said: "Hit me again Ike." Rolling on the river, that's where she would be.
Fletcher. *Liar, Liar.*

From the dead I am winning.
Sorceress Mab. *Merlin.*

Lessons Taught

95.

A memorandum is written not to inform the reader but to protect the writer.
Dean Acheson.

An oppressive government is more to be feared than a tiger.
Confucius.

Lessons Learned

Is there an echo here? Your objection's been recorded. She typed it into her little machine over there. It's on the record. So now, I'll proceed.
Ron Motley. *The Insider.*

Lessons Taught

96.

If any question why we died, tell them, because our fathers lied.
Rudyard Kipling. *Epitaphs of the War.*
Re: WWI, Kipling's only son

When your dreams turn to dust, it's time to vacuum.
Anonymous.

Lessons Learned

If history has taught us anything, it says you can kill anyone.
Michael Corleone. *The Godfather: Part II.*

My blood. Your blood. Our blood.
Sally Owen. *Practical Magic.*

Lessons Taught

97.

The individual is not a killer, but the group is and by identifying with it the individual is transformed into as killer.
Arthur Koestler.

Life is an echo; what you send out comes back.
Chinese Proverb.

Lessons Learned

_____
_____
_____
_____

You brought your kids to the court hearing?
Fletcher.
Sympathy.
Samantha.
Well, it's working. I feel sorry for them already.
Fletcher.
Liar, Liar.

Lessons Taught

_____
_____
_____
_____

98.

Society is frivolous and shreds its day into scraps, it's conversations into ceremonies and escapes.
Ralph Waldo Emerson.
Essays: Second Series, Character.

Those who have free seats at a play, hiss first
Chinese Proverb.

Lessons Learned

Is that legal?
Viceroy Knute Gunray.
I will make it legal. There is a question of procedure, but I'm confident we can overcome it.
Senator Palpatine.
The Phantom Menace.

Lessons Taught

99.

Loyalty to petrified opinions never yet broke a chain or freed a human soul.
Mark Twain. *Consistency.*

A donkey always says thank you with a kick.
Kenyan Proverb.

Lessons Learned

We're family. We're going to do a lot of dumb stuff together.
Tommy. *Tommy Boy.*

I always knew you would be drawn to your friends. Loyalty – highly overrated.
Albert Wesker. *Resident Evil: Afterlife.*

Lessons Taught

100.

All actions are judged by the motives prompting them.
Mohammad.

The thought, the dream, the vision, always precedes the act.
O.S. Marden.

Lessons Learned

_____
_____
_____

Stop it! You'll kill them.
Evelyn.
That's the idea.
Benji.
The Mummy.

Lessons Taught

_____
_____
_____

101.

In the name of certainty, the greatest crimes have been committed against mankind.
Carlos Fuentes.

Froth is not beer.
Dutch Proverb.

Lessons Learned

Death is ... whimsical ... today.
Stansfield. *The Professional.*

We struggle, we fight, we watch our friends die.
Alice. *Resident Evil: Afterlife.*

Lessons Taught

102.

At critical times the authorities always claim they have no authority or responsibility.
Anonymous.

Rats know the way of rats.
Chinese Proverb.

Lessons Learned

So, what do you mean "As it is written." Are you rewriting the whole thing, or just the parts that suit your needs.
Burt. *Children of the Corn.*

How rude.
Jar Jar Binks. *The Phantom Menace.*

Lessons Taught

103.

You can't wake a person who is pretending to be asleep.
Navaho Proverb.

Sincerity and truth are the basis of every virtue.
Lyman Abbott. *Problems of Life.*

Lessons Learned

Fahrenheit four-five-one is the temperature at which book paper catches fire and starts to burn.
Guy Montag. *Fahrenheit 451.*

She must destroy the evidence of her crime.
Atticus. *To Kill a Mockingbird.*

Lessons Taught

104.

Men are more apt to believe what they least understand.
Montaigne. *Essais.*

Fortitude is the guard and support of the other virtues.
John Locke. *Some Thoughts Concerning Education.*

Lessons Learned

You've got to learn about homicide. Why? Morons have committed murders so shrewdly that it's taken a hundred trained police minds to catch them.
Lt. Doyle. *Rear Window.*

Lessons Taught

105.

Almost all absurdity of conduct arises from imitation of those whom we cannot resemble.
Samuel Johnson. *The Rambler.*

If you don't stand for something, you will fall for anything.
Chinese Proverb.

Lessons Learned

You'll write this as a training accident.
Colonel Mekum. *Soldier.*

Stabbing went out with Bundy and Dahmer.
Anna. *The King and I.*

Lessons Taught

106.

A talent is formed in stillness, a character in the world's torrent.
Goethe. *Torquato Tasso.*

The greatest power that a person possesses is the power to choose.
J. Martin Kohe.

Lessons Learned

There are no victims, they're only being released.
Tom.
I see. A chance to save face.
Joan.
It Conquered the Earth.

Now you will experience the full power of the Dark Side.
Darth Sidious. *Revenge of the Sith.*

Lessons Taught

107.

There is a great deal of talk about loyalty from the bottom to the top. Loyalty from the top down is even more necessary and much less prevalent.
Gen. George S. Patton. *War As I Knew It.*

Lessons Learned

I'm suing God.
Steve Meyers.
The Church can only win if it proves God did not exist.
Anna.
The Man Who sued God.

Lessons Taught

108.

Is it progress if a cannibal uses knife and fork.
Stanislaw Lec. *Unkept Thoughts.*

Those who lie down with dogs, get up with fleas.
Benjamin Franklin. *Poor Richard's Almanac.*

Lessons Learned

After all he's just a Wookie.
C3PO. *The Empire Strikes Back.*

Let's get another Michael out of the warehouse.
Lou Craddock. *A Boy and His Dog.*

Lessons Taught

109.

The more uncivilized the man, the surer he is that he knows what is right and what is wrong.
H.L. Mencken. *Minority Report.*

Aiming isn't hitting.
Swahili Proverb.

Lessons Learned

What we do now echoes in eternity.
Maximus. *Gladiator.*

*¶I see a bad moon rising.
I see trouble on the way.¶*
Anna. *The King and I.*

Lessons Taught

110.

The hard fact is that violence breeds violence, and that, in turn, breeds insensitivity.
John Douglas and Mark Olshaker. *The Anatomy of Motive.*

A man is judged by his deeds, not by his words.
Russian Proverb.

Lessons Learned

You'd think at a certain point all these atypical somethings would amount to a typical something.
Dr. Sayer. *Awakenings.*

He who can destroy a thing, controls a thing.
Paul Atrides. *Dune.*

Lessons Taught

111.

When reality becomes unbearable, the mind must withdraw from it and create a world of artificial perfection.
Arthur Koestler. *The Sleepwalker.*

There is an old illusion. It is called good and evil.
Nietzsche.

Lessons Learned

The rules justify the means.
Danny.
The means is what you live with.
Nick.
The Corrupter.

Lessons Taught

112.

Remembrance wakes with all her busy train,
swells at my breast, and turns the past to pain.
Oliver Goldsmith. *Deserted Village.*

It is far harder to kill a phantom than a reality.
Virginia Wolfe.

Lessons Learned

We're doomed.
C3PO. *Star Wars.*

Well, Clarice – have the lambs stopped screaming?
Hannibal Lecter. *The Silence of the Lambs.*

Lessons Taught

113.

Fascism is not defined by the number of its victims, but by the way it kills them.
Jean-Paul Sartre. *Liberation.*

Every rope has two ends.
Kenyan Prover.

Lessons Learned

I personal would have looked for a more subtle solution, but that's not your way.
Monte. *Cobra.*

They're driven by that basest of impulses, the most basic needs.
Red Queen. *Resident Evil.*

Lessons Taught

114.

Washing one's hands of the conflict between the powerful and the powerless means to side with the powerful, not to be neutral.
Paulo Friere. *The Politics of Education.*

An ant on the move does more than a dozen ox.
Mexican Proverb.

Lessons Learned

Quick and easy is not how you run a multi-million-dollar business such as ours.
The Doctor. *Dr. Who.*

All we wanted was to enjoy what was left of our lives.
Velma. *Empire of the Ants.*

Lessons Taught

115.

It's always more pleasant to stone a martyr,
No matter how much we admire him.
John Barth.

The anvil fears the blow.
Romanian Proverb.

Lessons Learned

Deserve has nothing to do with this.
William Munny. *Unforgiven.*

You lost today kid; but, it doesn't mean you have to like it.
Roughrider. *Indiana Jones and the Last Crusade.*

Lessons Taught

116.

Actions speak louder than words, and they tell fewer lies.
Anonymous.

Listen and listen carefully: Opportunity often knocks softly.
Anonymous.

Lessons Learned

*¶Oh Danny boy, the pipes, the pipes are calling
From glen to glen, and down the mountain side
The summer's gone, and all the flowers are dying
'Tis you, tis you must go and I must bide.¶*
Danny Boy.

Lessons Taught

117.

To be remembered after we are dead is poor recompense for being treated with contempt while we are alive.
William Hazlitt. *Characteristics.*

A wound never heals enough to hide a scar.
Swedish Proverb.

Lessons Learned

*¶And I shall hear, tho' soft you tread above me.
And all my grave will warm and sweeter be
For you will bend and tell me that you love me
And I shall sleep in peace until you come to me.¶*
Danny Boy.

Lessons Taught

118.

Predators prey on the weak.
Edward Mazza. *Nevada Department of Corrections, Rano.*

Have a goal. A goal is a dream with a timeline.
Marjorie Blanchard.

Lessons Learned

Awful things happen in every apartment house.
Rosemary. *Rosemary's Baby.*

You were waving pompoms around this morning, and now you are a psychic hot line.
Scotty. *Jeepers Creepers.*

Lessons Taught

119.

It is by its promise of an occult sense of power that evil often attracts the weak. They hate not wickedness but weakness. When it is in their power to do so, the weak destroy weakness.
Eric Hoffer.
The Passionate State of Mind, and Other Aphorisms.

Lessons Learned

The bosses will do terrible things to me.
Jar Jar Binks. *The Phantom Menace.*

This is humanity's last stand. The beginning of the end.
Albert Wesker. *Resident Evil: Retribution.*

Lessons Taught

120.

> *Remember serial offenders are expert manipulators of other people.*
> Robert Ressler. *I Have Lived in the Monster.*

> *The liar needs good memory.*
> *Italian Proverb.*

Lessons Learned

> *You only get one life, and whatever you do with it, and whatever is done to you, you've got to face that. You can't pretend it didn't happen.*
> Cassie. *Murder by the Numbers.*

Lessons Taught

121.

Psychopaths suffer no qualm about the fate of their victims, and may even savor the pain they inflict.
Robert D. Hare. *Without any Conscience: The Disturbing World of the Psychopaths Among Us.*

Lessons Learned

It is in your nature to destroy yourselves.
The Terminator. *Terminator 2: Judgment Day.*

You'll get used to it… or you'll have a psychic episode.
Zed. *Men in Black.*

Lessons Taught

122.

All cruelty stems from weakness.
Lucius Annaeus Seneca. *Do Vita Beauta.*

When the eagles are silent, the parrots begin to jabber.
Winston Churchill.

Lessons Learned

I am altering the deal. Pray I don't alter it further.
Darth Vader. *The Empire Strikes Backs.*

She was half us, half something else. I wonder which was the predatory half,
Dr. Laura Baker. *Species.*

Lessons Taught

123.

Seldom would the subject direct his anger at the focus of his resentment.
John Douglas and Mark Olshaker. *Mind Hunter.*

Crooked wood is straightened with fire.
Sicilian Proverb.

Lessons Learned

Your mere presence should be motivation enough.
Professor Phipps. *Higher Learning.*

You had a son – We had a son. Since I could not kill you, my rage needed a victim.
Widow of the Web. *Krull.*

Lessons Taught

124.

The killer had the ability to hide his mental disease from co-workers or other people around him, this suggests average to above-average intelligence.
Robert Cullen. *Citizen X.*

Lessons Learned

That was no man. That was the Supreme Being.
Fidget.
You mean God?
Kevin.
Well, we don't know that him well, we only work for him.
Fidget.
Time Bandits.

Lessons Taught

125.

A technological advance and a social lag were responsible for the rise of the mercenary.
William Weir. *Fatal Victories.*

To him that watches, everything is revealed.
Italian Proverb.

Lessons Learned

Most scientists just play around with mice.
Dash. *Ice Spiders.*

They are closing us down, sending everyone to Auschwitz.
Amon. *Schindler's List.*

Lessons Taught

126.

Why inflict pain on oneself, when so many others are ready to save us the trouble.
George Pacaud. *Wickedness and Cruelty.*

The busy fly is in every man's dish.
Spanish Proverb.

Lessons Learned

You're supposed to be stupid, so don't abuse the privilege.
Braddock. *Blue Thunder.*

I've noticed an infestation here. Everywhere I look in fact.
Edgar/Bug. *Men in Black.*

Lessons Taught

127.

The one means that wins the easiest victory over reason: terror and force.
Adolf Hitler. *Mein Kampf.*

He who runs with wolves learns how to howl.
Spanish Proverb.

Lessons Learned

Serial killers get a sense of control from their killings.
Karen. *The Ugly.*

Ho help... No chance... No escape.
Sergeant Dobbs. *Without Warning.*

Lessons Taught

128.

The killer's anger was the focus of the assault.
Robert Keppel. Signature Killers.

His fantasies were of unlimited power and success.
Ray Hazelwood and Steven Michaud. Dark Dreams.

Lessons Learned

The problem with the serial killer is that after the first killing, however it was triggered, that motivation can disappear, and the killing itself becomes the purpose, because the killer enjoys himself and cannot stop... does not want to stop.
Stewart. Dead to Rights.

Lessons Taught

129.

Excess on occasion is exhilarating.
Somerset Maugham. *The Summing up.*

Children (nay, and men too) do most by example.
John Locke. *Some Thoughts Concerning Education.*

Lessons Learned

Is it usual for the host to kill a guest?
The Doctor.
In certain rarified circles.
Milton.
Dr. Who.

Lessons Taught

130.

Another improvement was that we built gas chambers to accommodate two thousand at a time.
Rudolf Hess. Nuremburg Trials.

A wise man changes his mind, a fool never will.
Spanish Proverb.

Lessons Learned

Perhaps I can find new ways to motivate them.
Darth Vader. Star Wars.

Who's the more foolish – The fool or the fool that follows him?
Ben Obi-Wan Kenobi. Star Wars.

Lessons Taught

131.

The great minds know very well that the object so treated, is an abstraction that is something of its reality has been lose.
C.S. Lewis. *The Abolition of Man.*

Once a thief, always a thief.
Italian Proverb.

Lessons Learned

Hey! Do you want to focus on the problem?
Zeus. *Die Hard with a Vengeance.*

I don't know what you're talking about. I don't feel any way at all.
Rhoda. *The Bad Seed.*

Lessons Taught

132.

*Educating the mind without educating
The heart is no education at all.*
Aristotle.

Birds of a feather flock together.
English Proverb.

Lessons Learned

I shall create power, and you will enforce it.
Barbara. *The Brain that Wouldn't Die.*

We do not discharge our weapons in view of the public.
Kay. *Men in Black.*

Lessons Taught

133.

In the war of ideas, it is people who get killed.
Stanislaw Lec. *Unkempt Thoughts.*

Anxiety never successfully bridges any chasm.
Giovanni Ruffinni.

Lessons Learned

Once you are able to kill mentally, the physical part is easy. The difficult part is to learn how to turn it off.
L.T. *The Hunted.*

Come little children I'll take thee away.
Sarah. *Hocus Pocus.*

Lessons Taught

134.

He might have proved a useful adjunct, if not an ornament to society.
Charles Lamb. *Captain Starkey.*

Every path has its puddles.
English Proverb.

Lessons Learned

You couldn't tell the parents from the kids until the old man lit up a cigar.
Archie Bunker. *All in the Family.*

It lives! It lives!
Dr. Frankenstein. *Young Frankenstein.*

Lessons Taught

135.

Repetition is reality, and it is the seriousness of life.
Kierkegaard. *Fear and Trembling, Repetition.*

The cost of liberty is less than the cost of repression.
W.E.B. Du Bois. *John Brown: A Biography.*

Lessons Learned

Once you familiarize yourself with the chains of bondage you prepare your limbs to wear them.
Rudy. *The Negotiator.*

Listen! I don't know who you are or where you come from but from now on you do as I tell you.
Princess Leia. *Star Wars.*

Lessons Taught

136.

> *Educating the mind without educating*
> *The heart is no education at all.*
> Aristotle.

> *Every soul is a battlefield.*
> Lyman Abbott. *Problems of Life.*

Lessons Learned

¶*Where have all the graveyards gone? Long time passing. Where have all the flowers gone? Long time ago. Young girls have picked them everyone, When will they ever learn?*¶
Peter, Paul and Mary. *Where Have All the Flowers Gone.*

Lessons Taught

137.

When, as he grows up, the plot thickens, and he puts on several shapes to act it.
John Locke. So*me Thoughts Concerning Education.*

The devil takes care of his own.
Scottish Proverb.

Lessons Learned

What are your expectations from this prison?
Winter. *The Last Castle.*

Unlike grown-ups, children have little need to deceive themselves.
Goethe. *Schindler's List.*

Lessons Taught

138.

Morality cannot be legislated, but behavior can be regulated. Judicial decrees may not change the heart, but they can restrain the heartless.
Rev. Martin Luther King, Jr.
Address to Western Michigan University.

Lessons Learned

Each generation will bear the burden in turn.
Arthur. *Merlin's Apprentice.*

Why should I feel sorry?
Rhoda. *The Bad Seed.*

Lessons Taught

139.

What this country needs are men with less bone in the head, and more in the back.
Anonymous.

Where there is a sea there are pirates.
Greek Proverb.

Lessons Learned

No, no. I'm anything but kind. In fact, I have a professional obligation to be malicious.
The Pitbull. *Babe: Pig in the City.*

Through them I will be invincible! My power will be absolute.
Kane. *Dr. Who.*

Lessons Taught

140.

Dependency invites encroachment.
Patricia Meyer Spacks.

Life shrinks or expands in proportion to one's courage.
Anais Nin.

Lessons Learned

She's not saying they killed him... just that maybe they shook his hand, and then he died...
Mysterious
Patty. *Practical Magic.*

Well, here's another nice mess you got me into.
Oliver Hardy. *Sons of the Desert.*

Lessons Taught

141.

***They would have propriety and possession,
pleasing themselves with the power.***
John Locke. *Some Thoughts Concerning Education.*

A spoon does not know the taste of soup.
Welsh Proverb.

Lessons Learned

I like being in charge. It's safer.
Sheila. *Exit to Eden.*

It's a praying mantis. She'll eat the rest of him.
Becky. *What's Eating gilbert Grape.*

Lessons Taught

142.

There are times when we are powerless to prevent injustice, but there should never be a time when we fail to protest.
Elie Wiesel. *Nobel Lecture, 11 December 1986.*

Old birds are hard to pluck.
German Proverb.

Lessons Learned

I helped the strangers conduct their experiments. I have betrayed my own kind.
Dr. Schreber. *Dark City.*

What turns a serial killer on is the suffering and death of another human being.
Helen Hudson. *Copycat.*

Lessons Taught

143.

There is nothing so eloquent as a rattlesnake's tail.
Navaho Proverb.

The only thing new in the world is the history you don't know.
Harry Truman.

Lessons Learned

We have to make them think it's for their own good.
Dr. Brodeus. *Miss Ever's Boys.*

I envy her happiness. I envy his happiness.
Laurie. *Little Women.*

Lessons Taught

144.

If everyone is thinking alike then someone isn't thinking.
Gen. George S. Patton. *War as I Knew It.*

The road to success is dotted with many tempting parking spaces.
Lyman Abbott. *Problems of Life.*

Lessons Learned

So, here's my question: What do we do when we find the answers we don't want.
Dr. Lessing. *The Substance of Things Hoped For.*

These doctors are savages.
Leo Getz. *Lethal Weapon 3.*

Lessons Taught

145.

A complex society is not necessarily more advanced than a simple one, it has just adapted to conditions in a more complex way.
Aristotle.

Where there are no swamps there are no frogs.
German Proverb.

Lessons Learned

The Empire will compensate you if he dies.
Darth Vader. *The Empire Strikes Back.*

These bodies are okay. They're like apartments we're just renting. But now we're movin' up.
Tiffany. *Bride of Chucky.*

Lessons Taught

146.

They just stared straight ahead with eyes that seemed to see nothing, and kept on following the man in front.
Fred Majdalany. *The Monastery.*

Our dog barks at something, the rest bark at him.
Chinese Proverb.

Lessons Learned

These bills are put together by legal minds after long study. Why I can't understand half of them myself and I used to be a lawyer.
Senator Joe Payne. *Mr. Smith Goes to Washington.*

It was routine.
Nazi Doctor. *Hitler's Henchmen: Mengele.*

Lessons Taught

147.

We think it is time that you recognized that you are masters in someone else's house. Despite the best intentions of the best of you, you must, in the nature of things, humiliate us.
Ghandi. *Ghandi.*

Lessons Learned

Once those droids take control of the surface, they'll take control of you.
Qui-Gon Jinn. *The Phantom Menace.*

The ceremony will be beautiful.
Shelby. Steel Magnolias.

Lessons Taught

148.

The public will believe anything as long as it is not founded on the truth.
Edith Stillwell. *Taken Care Of.*

Remember, even monkeys fall out of trees.
Korean Proverb.

Lessons Learned

A man who tells lies merely hides the truth. But a man who tells half-lies has forgotten where he put it.
Dryden. *Lawrence of Arabia.*

Evil twins.
Baron von Strucker. *Captain America: Winter Soldier.*

Lessons Taught

149.

We can deliberately harm other people to gratify ourselves.
Henry Flynt. *Self-Justification in Human Relations.*

Forbidden fruits make terrible jams.
Anonymous.

Lessons Learned

___

___

___

___

If they cannot find the truth, what is our hope of justice?
Rusty Sabich. *Presumed Innocent.*

And if you know what's good for you, you are going to love, honor, and obey.
Tiffany. *Bride of Chucky.*

Lessons Taught

___

___

___

___

150.

Every cook makes his own sauce.
French Proverb.

Cruelty hardens and degrades.
Robert Ingersoll. *What I want for Christmas*.

Lessons Learned

We're dealing with a very organized killer. He's someone who plans. His killings, they're not random spur of the moment things. He only kills who he wants to kill.
Ken O'Hara. *Bloodmoon*.

Lessons Taught

151.

Power never concedes anything without a demand. It never has and it never will.
Frederick Douglass. *West India Emancipation.*

A bad plowman quarrels with his oxen.
Korean Proverb.

Lessons Learned

Low risk victims, low risk areas. Everything very well planned. His behavior reflects his personality. His behavior is very well controlled, very well-orchestrated.
Ken O'Hara. *Bloodmoon.*

Lessons Taught

152.

If anything is sacred, the human body is sacred.
Walt Whitman. *I Sing the Body Electric.*

Quiet water splits a stone.
Bengali Proverb.

Lessons Learned

He's got a corporate secrecy agreement! Give me a break. I mean, this is a public health issue. Like an unsafe airframe on a passenger jet or some company dumping cyanide into the East River, issues like that!
Wallace. *The Insider.*

Lessons Taught

153.

Yet something may well be at work, when ritual is declared the Basic Social Act.
Catherine Bell. *Ritual Theory, Ritual Practice.*

After dark, all cats are leopards.
Zuni Proverb.

Lessons Learned

You're such a sucker for inspirational moods.
Ralph 'PaPa' Thorson. *The Hunter.*

She's on a rampage. We've got to warn the town.
Dr. Isaac Cushing. *Attack of the 50 Foot Woman.*

Lessons Taught

154.

The persecuting spirit has its origin... in the assumption that one's own opinions are infallibly correct.
John Fiske. *The Miscellaneous Writings of John Fiske.*

A hunter's knife does not carve its own handle
Korean Proverb.

Lessons Learned

Tataglia's a pimp. He never could have outfought Santino. But I didn't know until this day that is was - Barzini all along.
Don Vito Coreleone. *The Godfather.*

To celebrate death is a part of living.
David. *Candyman 3.*

Lessons Taught

155.

The chief source of man's humanity to man seems to be the tribal limits of his sense of obligations to other men.
Reinhold Niebuhr. *Man's Nature and His Communities.*

That is only the drop before the shower.
Irish Proverb.

Lessons Learned

In this courtroom, Mr. Miller, justice is blind to matters of race, creed, color, religion, and sexual orientation.
Judge Garrett.

With all due respect, your honor, we don't live in this courtroom, do we?
Joe Miller.
Philadelphia.

Lessons Taught

156.

Men have always liked to believe in their influence and direction in the course of time, these claims, however, sometimes conceal the truth.
Henry Hobhouse. *Seeds of Change.*

Lessons Learned

He really wants us to think what he's doing is an art. I think we are looking for someone desperate for acceptance... The murder is like a ritual. The method itself part of the pleasure.
Helen Hunt. *Copycat.*

Lessons Taught

157.

The vision that you glorify in your mind, the idea that you enthrone in your heart, this you will build your life by. This you will become.
James Allen. *As a Man Thinketh.*

All dreams spin out of the same web.
Hopi Proverb.

Lessons Learned

But as her bitterness grew the spell turned into a curse.
Aunt Francis. *Practical Magic.*

¶Show me the way to go home. I'm tired and want to go to bed.¶
Anna. *The King and I.*

Lessons Taught

158.

Man can certainly keep on lying, and does so, but he cannot hide the truth.
Karl Barth. *Church Dogmatics.*

The earth does not shake when the flea coughs.
Austrian Proverb.

Lessons Learned

For some warriors the answer is crystalized in an instant. Their instincts point them only one way. The truth becomes undeniable and – and apocalyptic.
Cogliostro. *Spawn.*

Lessons Taught

159.

What luck for rulers that men do not think.
Adolf Hitler.

Anyone can make mistakes. A fool insists on repeating them.
Robertine Maynard.

Lessons Learned

You, like your father, are now mine.
The Emperor. *Return of the Jedi.*

Circular logic only make you dizzy.
The Doctor. *Dr. Who.*

Lessons Taught

160.

Educating the mind without educating
The heart is no education at all.
Martin Burber. *Good and Evil.*

The summer insect knows not ice.
Japanese Proverb.

Lessons Learned

He'll be his father's son. Because of him the days of blood will go on and on, and out of it the people will come back to me. ~ Oh Merlin! From the dead I'm winning.
Sorceress Mab. *Merlin.*

Lessons Taught

161.

Facts do not cease to exist because they are ignored.
Aldous Huxley. *Proper Studies*.

Hell is truth seen too late.
Thomas Hobbes.

Lessons Learned

¶*When the postman delivered the letter,
It filled her heart full of joy.
But she didn't know till she read the inside,
It was the last one from her darling boy.*¶
Merle Haggard. *Soldier's Last Letter*.

Lessons Taught

162.

The great question (about power) is who should have it.
John Locke. *An Essay Concerning Human Understanding.*

Remember, one lie does not cost one the truth, but the truth.
Fredrich Hebbel,

Lessons Learned

The things that happened to me fifty years ago are more in my mind than the things that happened today. – Choose the things you'll be proud of and the things that last.
Grandma Lizzie. *Peggy Sue Got Married.*

Lessons Taught

163.

Half the truth is often a great lie.
Benjamin Franklin. *Poor Richard's Almanac.*

What worries you, masters you.
John Locke. *Attributed.*

Lessons Learned

After all they are emotionally inexperienced. We create a cushion, a pillow for their emotions and consequently we can control them better.
Dr. Eldon Tyrell. *Blade Runner.*

Lessons Taught

164.

When war is declared, truth is the first casualty.
Hiram Johnson.

Even paranoids have real enemies.
Delmore Schwartz. *In Falsehood in War.*

Lessons Learned

There is nothing like the safety of prestige.
Dr. Matt Hastings. *Tarantula.*

As long as you're under my roof things will be done my way.
Mary Fischer. *She-Devil.*

Lessons Taught

165.

He that scatters thorns, let him not go barefoot.
Benjamin Franklin.

Honesty is the first chapter of the book of wisdom.
Thomas Jefferson.

Lessons Learned

God didn't put man on earth to destroy his own kind, nor woman to enjoy agonies as they die.
Demetrius. *Demetrius and the Gladiators.*

The insurance company paid off.
Angelo. *Prizzi's Honor.*

Lessons Taught

166.

He urged his subjects to be what they were not and so prevented them from becoming what they might have been.
Jean-Jacque Rousseau. *The Social Contract.*

Propaganda, only propaganda is needed.
Adolf Hitler.

Lessons Learned

The only thing you have proven is that a woman in power can be every bit as abusive as a man ~ Do men deserve less?
Catherine Alvarez. *Disclosure.*

Your technique is not your weakness.
Morpheus. *The Matrix.*

Lessons Taught

167.

It is common for men to give pretended reasons instead of the real one.
Benjamin Franklin. *Poor Richard's Almanac.*

The obstacle is the path.
Zen Proverb.

Lessons Learned

I'm harvesting all these fantasies about some man I've never even met.
Annie Reed. *Sleepless in Seattle.*

They, they, they ~ I'm only paranoid because they want me dead.
Jerry Fletcher. *Conspiracy Theory.*

Lessons Taught

168.

Habits are safer than rules; you don't have to watch them. And you don't have to keep them either.
Frank Crane. *Essays.*

A fire is nourished by its own ashes.
Latin Proverb.

Lessons Learned

The accounts are confusing but they refer to an Inverse Exorcism, ~ The body is destroyed but the possessed soul remains.
Father Adams. *Vampires.*

Killing is an addiction like any other drug.
Tiffany. *Seed of Chucky.*

Lessons Taught

169.

Dare to be true; nothing can need a lie.
A fault, which needs it most, grow two thereby.
George Herbert. *The Temple.*

What has horns must not be put in a sack.
Zulu Proverb.

Lessons Learned

So, what do you mean what 'Should' is? And the only people who follow that are the people who do it because it is deemed socially acceptable.
Jerry. *Fall.*

Lessons Taught

170.

The most dangerous untruths are truths moderately distorted.
Lichtenberg. *Notebook 11.*

(Governments) tend to keep men children.
Henry Beecher.

Lessons Learned

This path will lead you to an unholy place.
Wiseman. *Army of Darkness.*

Your arrogance blinds you.
Darth Sidious. *Revenge of the Sith.*

Lessons Taught

171.

When a man lies, he murders some part of the world.
Rospo Pallenberg and John Boorman. *Excaliber.*

Moderation is a fatal thing. Nothing succeeds like excess.
Oscar Wilde.

Lessons Learned

You serve your Master well, and you will be rewarded.
Luke Skywalker. *Return of the Jedi.*

You don't know me, but a few years ago I killed your husband.
Tiffany. *Seed of Chucky.*

Lessons Taught

172.

Laws control the lesser man.
Right conduct controls the greater one.
Chinese Proverb.

A leopard does not change its spots.
Latin Proverb.

Lessons Learned

Go, since I need to die,
And give the world the lie.
Sir Walter Raleigh. *The Lie.*

We have to force his spirit into the grave.
Aunt Jet Owens. *Practical Magic.*

Lessons Taught

173.

Quality means doing it right when no one is looking.
Henry Ford.

You haven't failed until you quit trying.
Albert Einstein.

Lessons Learned

Truth is less fun than fiction.
Charlie Grimes. *High Crimes.*

You cannot escape your destiny. You must face Darth Vader again.
Ben Obi-Wan Kenobi. *High Crimes.*

Lessons Taught

174.

The least deviation of the truth is multiplied later a thousandfold.
Aristotle. *On the Heavens.*

It is easier to fight for one's principles than live up to them.
Alfred Adler. *Alfred Adler: Apostle of Freedom.*

Lessons Learned

Don't you know anything about Fantasia? It is the world of human fantasy. Every part, every creature of it, is a piece of the hopes and dreams of mankind. Therefore, it has no boundaries.
G'mork. *The NeverEnding Story.*

Lessons Taught

175.

Those who think it is permissible to tell white lies soon grow color blind.
Austin O'Malley. *Keystones of Thoughts.*

He that would not look forward must look behind.
Gaelic Proverb.

Lessons Learned

In a case like yours, an ounce of showmanship is worth a ton of evidence.
Kent. *The Women in His Life.*

Never hate your enemies. It affects your judgement.
Michael Coreleone. *The Godfather: Part III.*

Lessons Taught

176.

Try not to become a man of success but rather to become a man of value.
Albert Einstein. *Life Magazine.*

A bad workman never finds a good tool.
French Proverb.

Lessons Learned

Elementary, my dear Watson.
Sherlock Holmes. *The Adventures of Sherlock Holmes.*

Throughout time the battlefields have changed; but the price has always remained the same ~ the human soul.
Kevin Lomax. *Devil's Advocate.*

Lessons Taught

177.

Like all valuable commodities, truth is often counterfeited.
James Cardinal Gibbons. *The Faith of Our Fathers.*

Truth is truth to the end of reckoning.
William Shakespeare. *Measure for Measure.*

Lessons Learned

You don't know who you are anymore. Maybe it's time you investigated yourself.
Teddy. *Memento.*

He irked me. I should have left him alone.
Marie. *Innocent Blood.*

Lessons Taught

178.

The rights to do something does not mean that doing it is right.
William Safire. *No Uncertain Terms.*

The urge of destruction is also a creative urge.
Mikhail Bakunin.

Lessons Learned

This is a dangerous situation your Highness.
Captain Panaka. *The Phantom Menace.*

His crimes are of the most horrendous nature because he violated the trust of the public.
Dr. Michael Stone. *Most Evil.*

Lessons Taught

179.

The most terrifying words in the English language are: "I'm from the government and I am here to help you."
Ronald Reagan.

Lessons Learned

Let me be blunt: there is a labor crisis in America today.
Krusty.
Depends what you mean by "crisis."
George Meaney.
The Simpsons.

Lessons Taught

180.

Government is like a baby: An alimentary canal with a big appetite at one end and no sense of responsibility at the other.
Ronald Reagan.

Lessons Learned

They live in relationships and bribery.
Governor Trench. Lim jing dai yat gik.

Why should we give up any of that money? We had to kill two people to get it.
Mary. *Eating Raoul.*

Lessons Taught

181.

The children of the sun, ~ oh, how beautiful they were ~ They particularly dear to me ~ They were laughed at or pelted with stones.
Fyodor Dostoyevsky. *The Dream of a Ridiculous Man.*

Lessons Learned

Whatever is waiting for you out there, just know one thing: You are going to be in for the fight of your lives.
Jill. *Resident Evil: Afterlife.*

What good is a reward if you're not around to use it.
Han Solo. *Star Wars.*

Lessons Taught

182.

Nothing new happens in the world, for everything is but the repetition of the same primordial archetypes.
Mircea Eliade. *Myth of the Eternal Return.*

So, what compromises the Wild Woman? She is the Life/Death/Life force.
Clarissa Pinkola Estes. *Women Who Run with the Wolves.*

Lessons Learned

How am I going to make a report about this? If I say exactly what happened, they'll say I'm mad at headquarters.
Major de Bougolais. *Beau Jeste.*

Lessons Taught

183.

The happiness of your life depends upon the quality of your thoughts.
Marcus Aurelius. *Meditations.*

When you come to a fork in the road, take it.
Yogi Berra.

Lessons Learned

You must strive to You must strive to find your own voice.
John Keating. *Dead Poets Society.*

Of all the gin joints in all the towns in all the world, she walks into mine.
Rick. *Casablanca.*

Lessons Taught

184.

Waste no more time arguing about a good man should be. Be one.
Marcus Aurelius. *Meditations.*

The approach of demons to individuals may be commonly classed in three ways: Oppression, Obsession, and Possession.
John A. MacMillan. *Encounter With Darkness.*

Lessons Learned

We have locusts. There are locusts of all races and creeds. These, these locusts, incidentally are available at popular prices.
Fielding. *Bananas.*

Silly rabbit. Tricks are for kids.
O-Ren Ishii. *Kill Bill.*

Lessons Taught

185.

The soul becomes dyed with the color of its thoughts.
Marcus Aurelius. *Meditations.*

Belief is a moral act for which the believer is to be held responsible.
Lillian Hellman.

Lessons Learned

I think we better decide what brings out the best in humankind, and what brings out the worst, because it is either the stars or the jungle.
The Doctor. *Dr. Who.*

I see dead people.
Cole. *The Sixth Sense.*

Lessons Taught

186.

Two legal standards mean no legal standards.
Anonymous.

If it is not right do not do it; if it is not true don't say it.
Marcus Aurelius. *Meditations.*

Lessons Learned

_____
_____
_____
_____

Sometimes the truth sounds like a mouth full of worms.
Leonard. *North by Northwest.*

I'm mad as hell, and not going to take it any-more.
Howard Beale. *Network.*

Lessons Taught

_____
_____
_____
_____

187.

A room without books is like a body without a soul.
Cicero.

The best revenge is not to be like your enemy.
Marcus Aurelius. *Meditations.*

Lessons Learned

Many years ago, I was bitten by a werewolf. Now, whenever the full moon rises, I turn into a wolf myself
Larry Talbot.
That's alright. I'm a bit of a wolf myself.
Wilber Grey.
Bud Abbot and Lou Costello Meet Frankenstein.

Lessons Taught

188.

I be; You be; We be.
M.

Our life is what our thoughts make it.
Marcus Aurelius. *Meditations.*

Lessons Learned

I am a strong tree with branches for many birds. I am good for something in this world and I know it too.
The Doctor. *Dr. Who.*

I don't think her tree goes up all the way to the top of the branch.
Manfred. *Ice Age Meltdown.*

Lessons Taught

189.

Faith determines Belief.
Belief determines Faith.
M.

For those with faith, no evidence is necessary, for those without it, no evidence will suffice.
St. Thomas Aquinas.

Lessons Learned

One evil rises out of another.
Terence. *Eunuchus.*

Our technology has exceeded our humanity.
Sotascope. *Sentinel.*

Lessons Taught

190.

*The most powerful thing a society can do is
Is to have others adopt their religious ritual.*
M.

*He finds himself envying people who are protected
by the maternal embrace of an organization.*
Marie Louise von Franz, in C.G. Jung, Gen Ed.
Man and his Symbols.

Lessons Learned

*In a way you can't kill me.   'cause I died many,
many years ago.*
Beowulf. *Beowulf.*

Lessons Taught

191.

Spirituality is.
Theology explains.
Religion practices.
M.

There is nothing more frightening than ignorance in action.
Lyman Abbott. *Problems of Life.*

Lessons Learned

_____
_____
_____
_____

I find your lack of faith, disturbing.
Darth Vader. *Star Wars.*

I got a plan.
Earl. *Tremors*

Lessons Taught

_____
_____
_____
_____

192.

The things that we love tell us what we are.
St. Thomas Aquinas.

Judge not a horse by its saddle.
Chinese Proverb.

Lessons Learned

She's like a queen bee with a pick of the drones.
Jeff.
I say she is doing a woman's job: juggling the wolves.
Lisa. Rear Window.

Lessons Taught

193.

Mute sanction legalizes.
M.

Just as the twig is bent, the tree's inclined.
Alexander Pope.

Lessons Learned

Badges? We ain't got no badges! We don't need no badges! I don't need to show you any badges!
The Bandit. *The Treasure of Sierra Madre.*

I'll get you, my pretty, and your little dog, too!
Wicked Witch of the West. *The Wizard of Oz.*

Lessons Taught

194.

Lie to me, lie to me, tell me what I want to hear.
M.

It's deja-vu all over again.
Yogi Berra.

Lessons Learned

Listen to them. Children of the night. What music they make.
Count Dracula. *Dracula.*

Oh, no, it wasn't the airplanes. It was Beauty killed the Beast.
Carl Denham. *King Kong.*

Lessons Taught

195.

The socialized apocalyptic event is forced on the child.
M.

He who is not angry when there is just cause is immoral.
St. Thomas Aquinas,

Lessons Learned

Life is a banquet, and most poor suckers are starving to death.
Mame Dennis. *Auntie Mame.*

Carpe diem. Seize the day, boys. Make you lives extraordinary.
John Keating. *Dead Poets Society.*

Lessons Taught

196.

Sometimes we choose to suffer alone;
Sometimes we choose make others suffer with us.
M.

Self-mortification is not the path to enlightenment.
Buddha.

Lessons Learned

I'm the sheep that got lost.
Creasy. *Man on Fire.*

She got a whole Queen of the Undead thing going on.
Jay. *Men in Black.*

Lessons Taught

197.

The most noble part of medicine is knowing when to do nothing.
M.

Grass never grows again where my horse has once trodden.
Attila the Hun.

Lessons Learned

You build egos the size of cathedrals.
Milton. *The Devil's Advocate.*

Better to reign in Hell than serve in Heaven.
Kevin Lomax. *Devil's Advocate.*

Lessons Taught

198.

Ultimately, children judge parents.
M.

A forced kindness deserves no thanks.
Italian Proverb.

Lessons Learned

The wolf moves among the sheep.
Riddick.
The Chronicles of Riddick: Escape From Butcher's Bay.

Let's sheer them as the sheep they are.
Dark Warrior. *DragonHeart.*

Lessons Taught

199.

The psychological indicators of serial predators are similar to those of religious ritual.
M.

He who achieves power by violence does not truly become lord and master.
Thomas Aquinas.

Lessons Learned

So, this is how liberty dies... With thunderous applause.
Padme. *Revenge of the Sith.*
No.
Father Evert. *Daredevil.*

Lessons Taught

200.

Some rituals are adult games that should not be forced onto children.
M.

To love is to will the good of the other.
St. Thomas Aquinas.

Lessons Learned

What did I do to deserve this?
C3PO. *Attack of the Clones.*

What a gullible breed.
Kay. *Men in Black.*

Lessons Taught

www.ingramcontent.com/pod-product-compliance
Lightning Source LLC
Chambersburg PA
CBHW061638040426
42446CB00010B/1480